Ari '7ל6

INTRODUCTION TO
JEWISH
HISTORY
SEYMOUR ROSSEL

INTRODUCTION TO
JEWISH
HISTORY

SEYMOUR ROSSEL

ILLUSTRATED BY
KATHERINE KAHN

BEHRMAN HOUSE, INC.

ACKNOWLEDGMENTS

The author wishes to express his gratitude to the following people: Rabbi Manuel Gold, for assisting in the preparation of the maps throughout and for reading the materials relating to the biblical period. Dr. David Altshuler, for reading the materials relating to the post-biblical and Talmudic period. Their expertise was of enormous benefit; their friendship was sustaining. Mr. Adam Bengal, for helping to select and gather photographs from the four corners of the earth. Mr. Ralph Davis, who coordinated many efforts to create the final unification. And to my wife, Karen Trager Rossel, for styling the final manuscript, for her patience, and for her wisdom. S.R.

DESIGNED BY ROBERT J. O'DELL

MAPS BY JOSEPH ASCHERL

PHOTO CREDITS

American Heritage 13 / British Museum 12 / Brooklyn Museum 23, 39 / Davis, Ralph 40 / Harris, David 13 / Hoban, Tana 26, 95 / Israel Museum 38, 88, 97, 99 / Israel Office of Information 32, 100 / Jewish Museum 17, 20, 49, 75, 78, 86 / Lessing, Erich-Magnum 98 / Metropolitan Museum of Art 39 / Nowitz, Richard 19 / Pictorial-Crandall 94 / Radovan, Zev 84, 117 / Rossel, Seymour 70, 93 / University of Chicago 41, 52, 56

© COPYRIGHT 1981, BY SEYMOUR ROSSEL

PUBLISHED BY BEHRMAN HOUSE, INC.

MANUFACTURED IN THE UNITED STATES OF AMERICA

Library of Congress Cataloging in Publication Data
Rossel, Seymour.
Journey through Jewish history.
Contents: book 1 (From abraham to the sages.)
1. Jews—History—Juvenile literature. [1. Jews—History]
I. Title.
DS118.R592   909'.04924   81-3902
ISBN 0-87441-335-4 (v. 1)   AACR2

DEDICATION

For Amy and Deborah,
whose journey
is just beginning

Contents

IN THE DAYS OF THE BIBLE

UNIT ONE

1 Jewish History Begins   11
2 God Remembers Israel   15
3 The Great Covenant   20
4 The Promised Land   28
5 Israel Against the Philistines   35
6 The Kingdom and the Temple   40
7 The Northern Kingdom   46
8 The Kingdom of Judah   50
9 The End of Judah and the Temple   54
10 The Return to Jerusalem   58

IN THE DAYS OF THE RABBIS

UNIT TWO

11 Hellenism and Hasidism   66
12 Danger, Revolt, and Rome   71
13 Pharisees and Sadducees   76
14 Herod, King of the Jews   83
15 The Last Days of Judea   89
16 Old Ways and New   96
17 The Work of the Rabbis   102
18 Bar Kochba's Rebellion   107
19 Defeat and Victory   113
20 The Jews of Babylonia   118
21 Talmud: The Crowning Glory   122
Index   126

UNIT ONE

IN THE DAYS OF THE BIBLE

Long before the family of Abraham and Sarah came to the land of the Canaanites, history was well under way. Writing had been invented; priests and poets used it to tell of queens, kings, princes, and gods. The ships of the Island of Crete traded up and down the shores of the Mediterranean Sea. In China, the bamboo flute was invented; and the musicians of Egypt played on harps and lyres, and on the double clarinet. Human beings had invented the wheel, the weaving loom, the calendar of months and days, plows, and pottery. They wrote on clay or papyrus, made fine linen into sheets for their beds and fabric for their clothing, smelted gold and silver, made glass beads for jewelry, and watched and noted the movements of the stars in the heavens. Just about the time of Abraham and Sarah, human beings learned to use iron to make objects of metal.

1 JEWISH HISTORY BEGINS

Our Covenant   A special agreement marked the beginning of the history of our people. It was made first with Abraham, then with Abraham's son Isaac, then with Isaac's son Jacob, and finally with all of the people of Israel. But it began with Abraham.

In this agreement or *covenant*, Abraham was commanded to leave his home in Mesopotamia, to cross the river Euphrates, and to journey to the land of the Canaanites. He did so. He was commanded to name his son Isaac. He did so. He was commanded to circumcise his flesh and the flesh of every male born in his household as a sign of the covenant. He did so.

The other partner in this special covenant was not a human being or a nation. Abraham knew this partner by the name *El Elyon*, the God Most High. The Bible tells us that Abraham was not the first to know of this invisible God, of this God who demanded justice and mercy; but Abraham was the first to be chosen by God for a covenant, an everlasting covenant, a covenant for all times. God commanded:

> *I am God Almighty. Walk in My ways and be blameless. I will establish My covenant between Me and you, and I will make you exceedingly numerous . . . I will . . . make nations of you; and kings shall come forth from you . . . I will maintain My covenant between Me and you, and your offspring to come, as an everlasting covenant throughout the ages, to be God to you and to your offspring to come. I give the land you sojourn in to you and your offspring to come, all the land of Canaan, as an everlasting possession. I will be their God . . . As for you, you shall keep My covenant, you and your offspring to come, throughout the ages [Gen. 17: 1–9].*

Abraham and Sarah set out on the long journey that will become Jewish history. In the background is a *ziggurat,* a Mesopotamian pyramid.

The Bible tells us that Abraham came from Ur of the Chaldees. Archaeologists found a standard in that ancient city. It is called the "Standard of Ur." A powerful king receives gifts from many peoples. But whether this was the Ur of Abraham is still in question.

The God Most High Abraham came to believe that God was fair and loving. God had created human beings not, as the idol worshippers believed, so that they would serve God as a slave serves its master, but as a friend serves another friend. Yet the covenant was a sacred trust; Abraham undertook to do whatever was commanded of him.

The Bible tells that God commanded Abraham to sacrifice Isaac, his only son. Together, father and son climbed to the top of a mountain, taking with them the firewood and the knife for the sacrifice. As Abraham trusted God, so Isaac trusted his father. He did not complain as Abraham bound him and laid him upon the altar. Yet it was a test, a test and a lesson only. At the last moment God commanded Abraham not to harm Isaac, for the God Most High does not desire the sacrifice of human beings. Turning, Abraham saw a ram caught by its horns in the thicket. In grateful thanks to God who had spared his only son Isaac, Abraham offered up the ram as his sacrifice.

Jewish History Isaac's story is like the story of Jewish history. Time and again, the Jews have been tested; time and again, it has seemed that the Jewish people would be destroyed entirely by those who worshipped idols or worshipped no god at all; yet time and again, God has saved us and saved our covenant.

And this is the story we must tell, the story of Jewish history.

Idols were often made in molds. The mold in this photograph is an ancient one; the idol was cast from it only a few years ago.

IDOL WORSHIP AND MONOTHEISM

The ancient peoples were pagans. They believed that spirits or gods were all around them, helping and hurting them. They thought different gods ruled each part of nature—sun, moon, skies, land, and sea. And they thought human beings had been created as servants to the gods—to feed them and worship them.

Their gods were like themselves, as selfish and foolish as human beings can be. They were at war with one another, and they were pleased when human beings made war on one another to prove whose god was the greatest. The ancients built statues—idols —of their gods to keep in their homes and place in their temples; and they fed their gods by placing sacrifices—animals, and sometimes human beings, killed with great ceremony—before the idols.

Abraham began to spread a new idea. He taught that One God had created human beings—not as servants, but to be partners in the great work of creation. This One God could not be seen, nor could any idol be made in God's image. Abraham knew that God was the Ruler of the Universe; a just and merciful God; a God who did not wish for human beings to die, but to live together in peace. In time, Abraham's idea came to be known as *monotheism*, a Greek word meaning "belief in only one God." It is an idea which has changed history, a gift the Jewish people has shared with peoples all over the earth.

Ancient Egyptians worshipped many animals, among them this Hippopatamus goddess named Taureth. She looked after women during childbirth.

2 GOD REMEMBERS ISRAEL

From Freedom to Slavery The son of Isaac and Rebecca was Jacob, who was also called Israel. Jacob married two wives, Rachel and Leah; they had twelve sons and many daughters. They grew to be a tribe called the Hebrews or, sometimes, the Children of Israel. When there was hunger in Canaan, the Hebrew tribe moved to Egypt where Joseph, one of the sons of Jacob, had risen to a high place in the service of Pharaoh. The Pharaoh promised them a place to live, food to eat, and friendship. The tribe grew in size; and now they spoke of the twelve tribes of Israel. Generations passed, and there arose a new Pharaoh who did not remember Joseph and who broke the promises that had been made to the Israelites.

This new Pharaoh made the Israelites slaves. He forced them to labor in his fields, to make bricks of mortar and straw for his monuments and buildings, and to dig in his mines. Life was bitter for the Israelites; they were often beaten by the cruel taskmasters. The Bible tells us that the Lord God saw the hardships of the Israelites and remembered the covenant with Abraham. And, among the princes of Egypt, there was another who saw the hardships, too. This was Moses, adopted child of an Egyptian princess, who never forgot that he had been born a child of the Hebrew tribes.

Moses Leaves Egypt As he was walking once, Moses saw an Egyptian taskmaster whipping an exhausted Hebrew slave. Moses felt a terrible anger to

seph greets his brothers and welcomes
e Hebrew tribes to the land of Egypt.

Wall painting done in the time of Thutmose III shows slaves making bricks. One slave (far right) uses a plumb line to check that the walls are upright. This was the kind of forced labor the Hebrews suffered.

see one of his kinsmen suffer. He raised his arm and struck the Egyptian and killed him. Working quickly, Moses buried the dead man and hurried away. But the next day he learned that others had seen the murder. Pharaoh soon learned of the murder too and sent men to find Moses. But the Egyptian prince had fled into the desert, leaving behind him his life of ease and comfort.

He crossed the desert on foot, coming at last to the camp of Jethro, a priest of the Midianites. Moses took work as a shepherd for Jethro. He married one of Jethro's daughters, Zipporah. And he studied the ways of the desert peoples. He learned to find water where there seemed to be none; and food where none seemed to exist. In the future these lessons would be important as he led the Israelites through the wilderness.

The Burning Bush   On one journey as a shepherd, Moses came to Mount Horeb. There,

> *An angel of the Lord appeared to him in a blazing fire out of a bush. He gazed, and there was a bush all aflame, yet the bush was not consumed. Moses said, "I must turn aside to look at this marvelous sight; why is the bush not burnt?"* [Exod. 3:2–3]

Then Moses heard the voice of God calling to him from the bush. God commanded him to return to Egypt; to lead the Israelites to freedom.

Again Moses made the journey across the desert. With him was his brother Aaron, who would speak for him and help him. Moses was eighty years old and Aaron was eighty-three when they came before Pharaoh and ordered Pharaoh to let the Israelites go free. Pharaoh refused. The Torah tells how ten plagues were brought upon Egypt. After each one, Pharaoh agreed to let the Israelites go, only to change his mind again. But after the tenth, the harshest plague—death to the first-born sons of Egypt—Pharaoh begged Moses to take the Israelites and leave. For, among the firstborn, Pharaoh's own son had died.

The Exodus   Once a year, at the Passover Seder, we remember this great event, the *Exodus* (the "going out") from Egypt. In haste the Israelites made ready to leave. From the Egyptians they took silver, gold, jewelry as payment for their years of slavery. There was no time to bake bread, so they made dough and carried it on their backs where the desert sun soon baked it into flat unleavened cakes, *matzah*.

Meanwhile, Pharaoh had changed his mind again. He sent his chariots and warriors chasing after the Israelites to bring them back. Seeing the chariots approaching, the Israelites feared for their lives. But Moses commanded them to have faith in the Lord. He stretched out his arm, and the Lord opened the sea making a dry path for the Israelites to cross.

But when the chariots of the Pharaoh drove onto the dry path, their wheels were suddenly caught in mud, and

The name "Israel" is mentioned for what may be the first time on this *stele* or inscribed column. The victories of the Pharaoh Merneptah were recorded. (about 1220 B.C.E.).

On the map are two places marked *Sea of Reeds* and two marked *Mount Sinai* (?). For many years Bible scholars thought that the Hebrew tribes went south in Sinai before turning north again to Canaan. Today, most scholars believe that Mount Sinai was in the north and the Sea of Reeds mentioned in the Bible was a northern crossing.

the sea closed upon them, swallowing up horse, driver, and warrior alike. The armies of Pharaoh were destroyed.

The Israelites sang a song of victory. Moses' sister, Miriam the Prophetess, led the women in dance and song.

> *Sing to the Lord,*
> *For He has triumphed gloriously;*
> *Horse and driver*
> *He has hurled into the sea.* [Exod. 15:21]

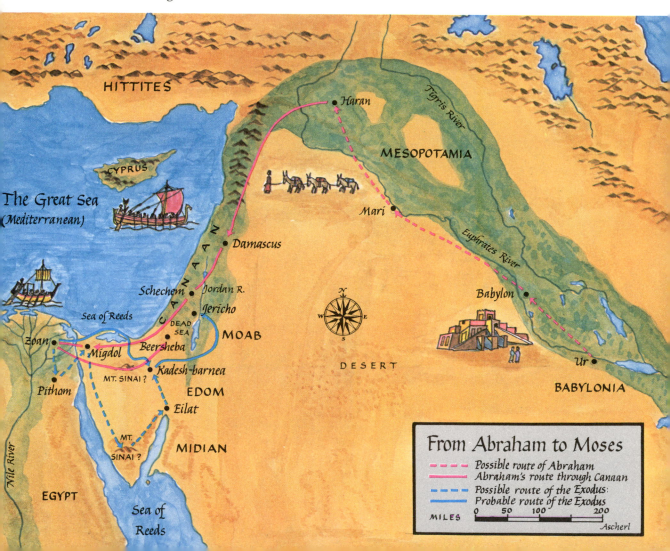

From Abraham to Moses

- - - - Possible route of Abraham
———— Abraham's route through Canaan
- - - - Possible route of the Exodus
———— Probable route of the Exodus

MILES 0 50 100 200

Ascherl

MOSES IN EGYPT

We know the story of Moses from the Torah, the first five books of the Bible, which tells us little about the life he led as an Egyptian prince. But we can imagine what that life may have been like since historians and archaeologists have learned much about ancient Egypt and the Pharaohs.

If Moses was truly an Egyptian prince, he must have studied with other princes at the Egyptian temples. There the priests taught him to read the picture signs called hieroglyphs, the alphabet and writing symbols of the Egyptian kingdom. He studied penmanship, using a reed pen on papyrus paper, and ink made of charcoal and gum. He memorized long poems and lists of Pharaohs and their wars. He wore a linen loincloth and belt and a jeweled sword; he rubbed his body with perfumes and oils; and he may have worn the jewelled collar of the Egyptian royal princes. As a young man, he studied how to command an army, how to hunt, and how to lead people. Yet he must have felt a little out of place in this rich Egyptian world, for he knew that he was born an Israelite.

Egyptians believed that life after death was as important as the present life. They also believed it was so much like present life that one could take belongings to the next world. They glorified death by building grand tombs such as the pyramids, and decorating the inside rooms with great works of art and writing.

3 THE GREAT COVENANT

The Beginning of the Journey   The people moved slowly through the wilderness. There were times of hunger and thirst. But Moses told them to have faith in the Lord. One morning the dew fell; and when the dew was gone, there was *manna*. It was food like the coriander seed, but it tasted like wafers made with honey. The Israelites gathered it that day and for as long as they wandered in the wilderness.

But it troubled the people that there were no rules for them to follow. To Moses they brought every argument for settlement. Jethro saw this. He warned Moses that no person could have strength enough to listen to every argument. He told Moses to choose honest men to be chieftains for the people—chieftains who would listen to the people and bring only the most important matters to Moses. That is what Moses did.

THE SINAI WILDERNESS.
In this harsh terrain,
the Hebrew tribes
became one people
united in the belief in
the One God.

What Happened at Sinai The Israelites now camped at the foot of Mount Horeb, which also is called Mount Sinai. Something happened there that changed history for all time. God spoke to the Israelites and made a covenant with them. Tradition tells us that God gave Moses the Torah there, laws for all the peoples of the earth to live by. Amid thunder and the calls of the ram's horn, and in the midst of lightning and fire, the great covenant was made between God and the people.

Ten commandments of God were inscribed on two stone tablets that Moses brought down from the mountaintop. In the forty days and forty nights that Moses spent on the mountain, he had learned much of God and God's ways. In the years to come he taught the people what he had learned: that the world was based on a plan which is fair and just, created by a God who is fair and just; and that the plan of creation was Torah. The laws of Torah are laws for all time; and God's promises to Israel are promises for all time. It is an everlasting covenant.

The Golden Calf As Moses carried the two stone tablets down the mountainside to his people, his face shone with the brightness of heaven. But when he saw what had happened while he was gone, the brightness turned to anger. The Israelites had brought gold to Aaron; and Aaron had cast the gold into the shape of a calf. And now the Israelites were bowing to the idol and worshipping it. Moses hurled the tablets of the covenant to the ground, smashing them to pieces.

Seeing Moses' anger, the people were ashamed. They knew they had done wrong; they had broken God's law—a law they had possessed for only forty days. For they had been commanded:

> *You shall not make for yourself a sculptured image, or any likeness of what is in the heavens above, or on the earth below, or in the waters under the earth. You shall not bow down to them or serve them. [Exod. 20:4–5]*

Moses burnt the golden calf and destroyed it. When his anger passed, he climbed the mountain again, returning with two more stone tablets. These he placed in a small wooden chest called the Ark of the Covenant. Now when the Israelites marched, the priests marched before them, carrying the Ark of the Covenant on poles.

Carrying the Ark of the Covenant.

The mosaic floor of an early synagogue shows one of Judaism's first symbols, the seven-branched menorah.

SANCTUARY AND PRIESTS

The Book of Exodus tells how God commanded Moses to have the people bring together their riches and their finery to make a portable building for worship. The Lord said, "Let them make Me a sanctuary, that I may dwell among them." [Exod. 25:8]

For months the Israelites worked to build the Lord's sanctuary. They made it of cloth and wood, covered it with gold, silver, and bronze. The Israelite artist Bezalel made a golden seven-branched menorah for the sanctuary, and an altar. Then, when all was ready, Moses sacrificed a lamb and a bull on the altar.

Never again did Moses offer a sacrifice there, for it was Aaron and his sons who were chosen to be the priests of Israel, to offer up the sacrifices of the people.

The Spies   In a while, the Israelites reached Kadesh-barnea, an oasis near the edge of the wilderness, just fifty miles from the Promised Land, Canaan. Now Moses chose twelve men from among the tribes. He sent them as spies into Canaan to see the land and its people. When the spies returned, they carried figs and pomegranates; and bunches of grapes so huge that two men had to carry them on poles upon their shoulders. The land was truly "flowing with milk and honey." But ten of the spies said it could not be conquered. The cities were too strong, they reported, and the people in them were giants. Only Joshua and Caleb believed that the cities could be taken. But the people believed the ten spies and were afraid.

So Moses kept the people at Kadesh-barnea. The old generation—those born in slavery in Egypt, all except Joshua and Caleb—died there in the wilderness. Moses grew older, too; and he lost his patience. When the

THE SPIES RETURN. Of the twelve, only Joshua and Caleb thought the land could be conquered.

people complained there was no water, he struck a rock to make water flow, when God had told him just to speak to it. It was then that Moses knew the people needed a new leader.

The Death of Moses   When he saw the old generation had passed, Moses led the people to the edge of Canaan. There he repeated the words of Torah so that all might hear; and the scroll of the Torah he placed in the Ark. He told Joshua to be strong and to lead the people well. Then he climbed to the top of Mount Nebo and looked over into the Promised Land, the land he could not enter. Moses was one hundred and twenty years old when he died there, and the Israelites mourned him for thirty days. "Never again," the Torah says, "did there arise in Israel a prophet like Moses, whom the Lord singled out, face to face . . ." [Deut. 34:10]

Mt. Sin

Modern scholars argue that Mount Sinai is really far to the north (see map, page 18); but through the centuries pilgrims have come to this ragged mountaintop, believing that this is the true Mount Sinai.

THE TEN COMMANDMENTS

Abraham gave the Jewish people the idea of *monotheism*, belief in the One God. When Moses brought the tablets of the law down from Mount Sinai, a new idea was born—the idea of *ethical monotheism*. The One God had given human beings commandments or "ethics," standards by which to live. These are the ten commandments which the Bible tells us were written "by the finger of God" on the tablets of stone:

I am the Lord your God who brought you out of the land of Egypt, the house of bondage. You shall have no other gods before Me.

You shall not make for yourself a sculptured image, or any likeness of what is in the heavens above, or on the earth below, or in the waters under the earth. You shall not bow down to them or serve them. For I the Lord your God am an impassioned God, visiting the guilt of the fathers upon the children, upon the third and upon the fourth generations of those who reject Me, but showing kindness to the thousandth generation of those who love Me and keep My commandments.

You shall not swear falsely by the name of the Lord your God; for the Lord will not clear one who swears falsely by His name.

Remember the sabbath day and keep it holy. Six days you shall labor and do all your work, but the seventh day is a sabbath of the Lord your God; you shall not do any work—you, your son or daughter, your male or female slave, or your cattle, or the stranger who is within your settlements. For in six days the Lord made heaven and earth and sea, and all that is in them, and He rested on the seventh day; therefore the Lord blessed the sabbath day and hallowed it.

Honor your father and your mother, that you may long endure on the land which the Lord your God is giving you.

You shall not murder.

You shall not commit adultery.

You shall not steal.

You shall not bear false witness against your neighbor.

You shall not covet your neighbor's house; you shall not covet your neighbor's wife, or his male or female slave, or his ox or his ass, or anything that is your neighbor's.

4 THE PROMISED LAND

About the Canaanites   The people who lived in the land God promised to the Israelites were called Canaanites. They were warriors. They fought with sword and bow; and they owned chariots of iron. They carried heavy shields of leather covered with metal; and they wore armor made of iron. Their armies were fast and strong on the plains and in the flat countryside, but in the hills the wheels of the chariots broke upon the rocks and the soldiers' armor made climbing slow and difficult.

Battling the Canaanites.

The Israelites Under Joshua   The Israelites had become good fighters under the leadership of Moses and Joshua. They wore little armor and carried light shields made mostly of leather, and they fought with hand weapons—the spear and the axe, the slingshot and the short sword. Joshua knew that the Israelites were no match for the armies of Canaan on the plains where the chariots could ride them down and hunt them. But in the hills the armies of Israel were quick and able. So Joshua led his people into the hills first; and the Canaanites were driven from the hills.

The Judges   After Joshua's death, new leaders arose among the people Israel. They were called judges, though in truth they were more often generals. Each judge ruled for a short time, usually over one tribe. One of the most famous of the judges was Deborah who led many tribes against the king of Hazor and his general Sisera. Deborah chose a general from among the Israelites, a man named Barak. But Barak was afraid to lead his men into battle, so Deborah and Barak together led the charge and defeated the enemy. One enemy was defeated, but still others came against Israel.

At harvest time, the fierce camel-riding people called Midianites stole the grain from the Israelites' threshing floors. Against these raiders, the judge Gideon led three hundred chosen farmers. He gave each of them a torch, an empty pitcher, and a shofar. In the middle of the night, the Israelites encircled the sleeping camp of Midian. All at once they blew on the horns, broke the pitchers, and lit their torches. The camp was in sudden confusion. The Midianites thought they were surrounded by a great enemy. In the dark they fell on one another, killing their own people; and Gideon and his men killed many more Midianites as they fled.

The land of Canaan was divided among the tribes of Israel, and then each family was given a portion.

THE CANAANITES

The Canaanites were not one people, but many. Most lived in walled cities up and down the countryside, each with its own ruler and its own laws. They worshipped many gods. They spoke of the "old" god, El, the kindliest of the gods, the father of the gods, the creator; and of the "young" god, Baal, who ruled the fields, sent the rain, and rode the clouds. When the rain was slow in coming, they offered sacrifices to the idols of Baal; and when a couple had no children, they offered sacrifices to the idols of Astarte, the Canaanite goddess of love.

A Canaanite walled city.

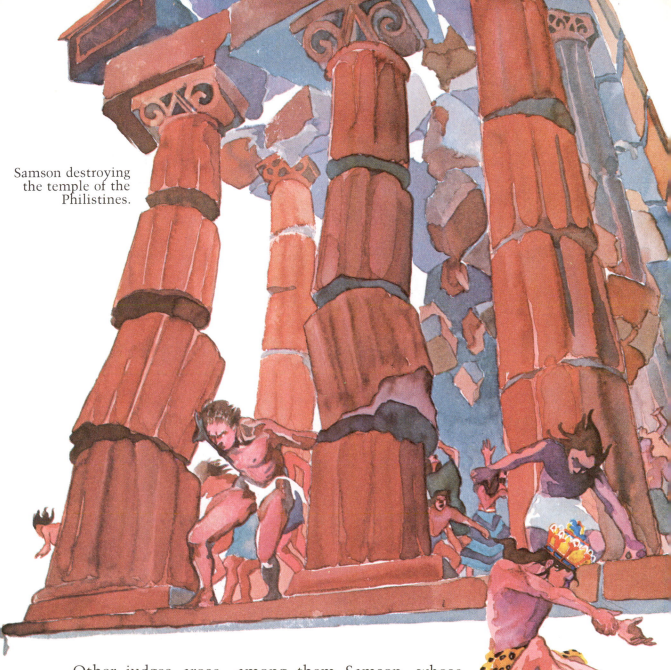

Samson destroying
the temple of the
Philistines.

Other judges arose—among them Samson, whose
strength was so great that people said he once killed a
thousand Philistines with the jawbone of a donkey. Even
after he was captured by the Philistines and his eyes were
put out so that he was blind, he was so strong that he
pressed apart two columns of the Philistine temple to

bring the roof down upon himself and all the Philistines who were in it. That day, the Bible tells, he killed more Philistines as he died than he had in all the days of his life.

Because They Forgot the Covenant
For two hundred years the battles continued between Israel and the Canaanite peoples; and at times the Israelite tribes even fought among themselves. Yet one thing united them: the covenant they had made with the Lord. Joshua had reminded them of this covenant when the Israelites built a sanctuary at Shiloh. Here the tribes came together to worship God and to talk over their problems. Here, too, was kept the Ark of the Covenant, Israel's greatest possession.

As time passed, however, the memory of the covenant began to fade. It was easy for the people to follow the ways of the Canaanites. Slowly they came to believe that to bring rain they had to worship the god Baal, and to have children they had to worship the goddess Astarte. The judges warned them that God would punish their idolatry, but the people were stubborn and did not listen.

Disaster came when the Philistines joined together to attack the Israelites around the year 1050 B.C.E. The Israelites brought the Ark of the Covenant from Shiloh and placed it where all could see it. But the battle was lost; and the Ark was taken captive by the Philistines. The priests

This stone carving from a 1st century synagogue shows what the Ark of the Covenant may have looked like. Here it is seen on an ox-cart, as it may have been when it was captured by the Philistines.

from Shiloh who had brought the Ark were killed; and a short time later the tabernacle at Shiloh was destroyed.

The people of Israel were sore afraid. There was no king to guide them, and no general to command them. No doubt the Israelites wondered if God had forgotten them; and even the darkness of the night must have seemed darker in those days.

THE JUBILEE YEAR

When the Israelites settled in the land of Canaan, the land was split up among the tribes and a piece of it given to each family. Just as human beings were commanded by God to rest every seventh day on the Sabbath, God commanded that the land be allowed to rest every seventh year. This was the Sabbatical Year, called *Shemitah* in Hebrew. In that year no farming was done, and the people lived on the grain that grew wild in the fields.

Seven times the people were to observe the year of Shemitah, and the next year, the fiftieth year, on the day of Yom Kippur, the ram's horn was blown to announce the coming of the year of Jubilee or *Yovel*. In the Jubilee Year, too, the land was rested and no work done on it. But the Jubilee was special for other reasons, too. In that year all slaves were freed; and any family that had sold its land during the past forty-nine years had its land returned. In this way, God's commandments provided that the land would always belong to the tribes of Israel, and the families would never grow so poor that they would not share in God's promised land.

Carchemish •   • Haran

CYPRUS

Tiphsah •

Arvad •   Hamath •

H A M A T

Gebal •   Lebo-hamath •   Tadmor •

Euphrates River

Tyre •   Damascus •

The Great Sea
(Mediterranean)

Jordan R.

Rabbath-bene-ammon •

Jerusalem •

Gaza •   Karkar •

Brook of Egypt

Eilat •

EGYPT

The Kingdom in the days
of Solomon

about 990-928 B.C.E.

0   50   100   150 MI.

Ascherl

5 ISRAEL AGAINST THE PHILISTINES

The War Continues   The Ark of the Covenant was in the hands of the Philistines, but it brought them only bad luck. In the end, they came to fear it; and they sent it back to the Israelites on a wooden cart. But just having the Ark did not bring victory to the Israelites. For twenty years the war continued and it seemed that the Philistines might win.

But the Israelites found a new leader, the Judge Samuel. Like the judges before him, Samuel led his people into battle. But he was a new kind of judge, too. He traveled from tribe to tribe, listening to the arguments between the Israelites, and judging them as modern judges do. And he was a prophet. The people believed that Samuel could speak with God and tell them what God wanted.

Saul, first king of Israel.

Give Us a King As time passed and the war against the Philistines went on, the people grew tired, and Samuel grew old. At last, the leaders of all twelve tribes came to him. "Give us a king," they said. But Samuel warned them: "God is your King. A human king will force you to serve in his army, he will make you slaves, and he will take away your lands." Nevertheless, they said, "Give us a king to judge us like the other nations."

Then Samuel went to the tribe of Benjamin, the smallest tribe, and found a man named Saul. Like most Israelites, Saul was a farmer. But he was tall and handsome, and Samuel felt that he was the right man to be king. So the prophet took a cup of perfumed oil and poured it over Saul's head, and with this he made Saul king of Israel.

At first things went well for Saul. He listened to Samuel and he won battles against the Philistine enemy. But then he grew to believe that he could win without Samuel, and things began to go badly. Samuel turned away from him; and Saul grew more and more troubled. At times his temper rose so that he could not control it.

Samuel chose a new king without telling the people.

This new king was David the son of Jesse from the tribe of Judah, Israel's largest tribe. When Saul's family looked for a harpist to play for the king and to sing sweet songs to soothe the king in times of trouble, lo and behold, the man they found was the very same David. So it came to pass that David, who was to be the next king of Israel, came to Saul's tent.

David was well-liked by all. The people began to say

of him, "Saul has slain thousands of Philistines, but David has slain tens of thousands." This made Saul more and more jealous of David. The time came when Saul tried to kill David; and David was forced to flee.

David the King   David gathered around him a small group of warriors from the tribe of Judah. And he waited. He and his warriors camped near the Philistines and studied their ways. Saul grew ever more troubled, and sent his men out to find David to kill him; but in the end it was Saul and his son Jonathan, who had been David's best friend, who were killed in a battle against the Philistines.

David celebrates his victories.

Now the people turned to David and made him king. In the south, among the tribes of Judah and Benjamin, David became king upon Saul's death. But it took seven years before the tribes in the north accepted him as their leader. Now David defeated the Philistines and made a covenant with them, so that they would serve him.

David captured the Jebusite city of Jerusalem and made it his capital. There he built a small tabernacle and brought to it the Ark of the Covenant. Many other Canaanite cities made covenants with David, until the land of Canaan was truly one kingdom. David sent his warriors across the Jordan River to the east where he conquered the lands of Ammon, Moab, and Edom, and made a covenant with the Arameans.

Part of a clay tablet telling the story of Gilgamesh, the earliest tale of the Great Flood. The words are formed in cunieform, each symbol pressed into the clay while it was still soft. When it was complete, the clay tablet was baked to harden and preserve it.

THE STORY OF THE ALPHABET

North of Israel, in the land called Lebanon, lived a people that the Bible called, "the merchant of the peoples . . ." The Greeks called them Phoenicians, the name by which we know them today. The Phoenicians were mighty builders. Their port cities —Tyre, Byblos, Ugarit, and others—were filled with beautiful and impressive buildings; and their ships—made of cypress and cedar woods, with oars of oak—were famous throughout the ancient world.

The Phoenicians traded in wine and grains, in carved ivories from Egypt and fine pottery from Greece, in spices and in coral. But their most precious cargo was cloth dyed a deep crimson shade. This colorful cloth was used to make robes for kings and princes, and gowns for princesses and queens. Only the wealthiest could afford it, for the making of the dye and the dyeing of the cloth were done by hand. The color gave the people its name, for in Greek the word *Phoenicia* means "land of purple."

Both the Phoenicians and the Israelites changed history. The Israelites did this through their teachings about the idea of the One God, merciful and just, who rules over all. The Phoenician traders did this by spreading another idea—the idea of the alphabet.

Inscription found on the southwestern corner of the Temple mount in Jerusalem. The first two words read: לבית התקיעה "To the place [house] of trumpeting . . ."

Clay tablet containing Egyptian hieroglyphs.

Writing began as pictures. A picture of a house meant "house." Later, the Egyptians began to use some of their pictures as syllables. So the picture of a certain bird can mean that bird or the syllable "nh." This Egyptian picture and syllable writing is called *hieroglyphic.* The Canaanites used pictures for their beginning sound or consonant. So the picture of a house *bayt,* became the symbol ב for the sound of "b." A picture was now a "letter." The Phoenicians added their own idea to this. They listed their letters and used only 22 of them. This was an *alphabet.* Wherever the Phoenician ships went, they taught their alphabet; and the Hebrews learned it,

The Hebrews settled on 22 letters of their own and created the *alef bet.* Like all ancient writing in the Near East, their line began on the right and read to the left; and they used the same alef bet for writing the two languages which they spoke—Hebrew and Aramaic.

This document was written in Hebrew letters, but the language is not Hebrew, but Aramaic. Aramaic was spoken as the daily language of the Jews in Israel.

Looking up from the desert below at one of the Pillars of Solomon. Copper ore was mined in the shadows of these ancient cliffs in the time of the kings.

6 THE KINGDOM AND THE TEMPLE

The Kingdom of David From Egypt to Mesopotamia, the Promised Land was ruled by the Israelites at last. Now David began to create a government for it. He appointed a scribe to take down in writing everything that happened, and a man to announce new laws to the people. He appointed two high priests in Jerusalem to offer sacrifices to the Lord, and then appointed governors and judges for the many parts of the kingdom.

Yet not all was peaceful at home. Once when David was away from Jerusalem, Absalom his son tried to become King. In the battle between David's warriors and Absalom's followers, Absalom was killed. Then another son rose up against David. And this rebellion, too, David crushed. Finally, following the advice of the prophet, Nathan, David chose his son Solomon to be the next king of Israel.

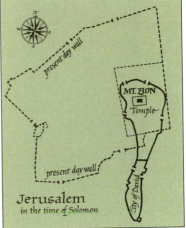

Solomon—Third King of Israel   Of all David's sons, Solomon was the wisest. When David died, Solomon made treaties with Egypt and other countries, and the land of Israel grew rich. From his friend Hiram, king of Tyre in the land of the Phoenicians, Solomon borrowed many craftsmen and builders. With their help he strengthened the walls and cities of Megiddo, Gezer, and Hazor; and he built a new port city on the Gulf of Eilat, called Etzion-geber. Near this city, Solomon's slaves mined copper for their king; and with his new riches Solomon built many ships, hired sailors from the Phoenicians, and brought to Israel cargoes of gold, precious stones, ivory, and spices.

Solomon came to the throne in 961 B.C.E. and ruled until his death in 922 B.C.E. Far and wide he was known as a great king, a wise king, and a powerful king.

Canaanite altar for burning incense. The points at the four corners were called "horns." There were horns like these on the altar in the Temple.

The Temple   But the greatest of his triumphs was the building of the Temple in Jerusalem, a new and glorious House of the Lord, in which he placed the Ark of the Covenant. Fine cedar trees were brought from Lebanon to make the pillars of the Temple; and much gold and many precious stones were used in its decoration. When it was complete, Solomon dedicated it.

It was a time of peace. David had brought Canaanite musicians to play at his court, and to compose new music for his tabernacle; now Solomon made music a part of the Temple service. Choirs sang the songs of

David and psalms were played on many instruments—drum, lyre, harp, flute, bells, and trumpets. And Solomon brought writers to compose new poetry for his court. This new kind of poetry, called "wisdom literature," gave rise to some of the books of the Bible—Proverbs, Job, Song of Songs, Ecclesiastes.

Life on the Land   An ancient calendar, found at Gezer, tells what farm life was like for the people from one autumn to the next:

THE WISDOM OF SOLOMON
Solomon was known far and wide as the wisest king of his time. To show how great was his wisdom, the Bible tells this story.

Once two women came before the king. Both had become mothers on the same night, but the child of one had died. In the night, the woman whose child had died stole the child of the other woman, leaving behind the body of her own, dead child. Now the two argued over whose child was the living one. But how would the king, who knew neither of them, decide?

The king said, "Bring a sword and divide the living child in half; and give one part to each." The real mother said, "O my lord, give the child to her, but do not kill it!" But the other woman said, "No, it shall be neither thine nor mine; divide it!" At that, Solomon knew which was the true mother. And the king gave the child back to its real mother. The Bible ends the story, saying, "All Israel heard of the judgment which the king had judged; and they respected the king; for they saw that the wisdom of God was in him, to do justice."

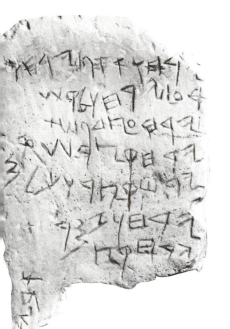

The Gezer calendar of the 10th century B.C.E. recorded information to farmers as to when to plant and harvest their crops.

Two months of [olive] harvest,
  Two months of planting [grain],
    Two months of late plantings;
One month of hoeing flax,
  One month of harvesting barley,
    One month of harvest and storing;
Two months of tending [grape] vines,
  One month of the summer fruit.

Excitement came three times a year as many Israelites journeyed to the Temple in Jerusalem to offer sacrifices. They came on Sukkot to celebrate the harvest; on Passover to celebrate the spring and remember the exodus from Egypt; and on Shavuot to celebrate the first fruits of summer.

These were the years of Israel's glory; and Solomon was the most glorious of Israel's kings. After him there would be quarreling and division, but for now the people lived in peace; and their faith in God—the God of Abraham, Isaac, and Jacob—grew. For God had promised them that they would inherit the land, and that the land would flow with milk and honey; and all that God promised had come to pass.

DAVID AND GOLIATH. Few Israelites had swords and the slingshot was a popular weapon, especially among shepherds who used it to protect their flocks from wild animals.

THE ROYAL LINE OF DAVID

Because the kingdom of Israel rose to greatness under David, he became a beloved hero of the Jewish people. He was the great warrior who had slain the giant Goliath and defeated the Philistines in battle. He was the great builder who had founded his capital in Jerusalem and built his palace there. Jerusalem was called "The City of David."

Yet David came from simple folk. His father was Jesse of Bethlehem, a shepherd. And his great-grandmother was Ruth whose story is told in the Bible. Ruth was one of two Moabite women who married the sons of Naomi the Israelite. And when both sons died, and Naomi decided to return to the land of the Israelites, the loyal Ruth decided to go with her. "Your people shall be my people," Ruth said to her mother-in-law; and the two journeyed to Israel together. In Israel, the story had its happy ending, for Ruth the convert met and married Boaz, a kindly farmer and a relative of Naomi. We read the story of Ruth each year in the synagogue on the holiday of Shavuot, for it was harvest time when Ruth and Boaz met.

Perhaps the faithfulness of Ruth was a part of David's family heritage, for the Bible tells how God promised that the throne of Israel would always belong to a child of the family of David. This covenant between God and David gave rise to a new belief among the people. It was said that in the end of days, a new king, the Messiah, would be anointed with oil—the word Messiah means "the anointed one"—and would rule over all the peoples of the world in peace. And, because of God's promise, the Messiah would come from the royal line of David.

To this very day, in our prayers, we ask for the rebuilding of the city of Jerusalem and the coming of the Messiah, the offspring of David.

Ruth gleans in the fields of Boaz. Gleaning was an early form of *tzedakah*. The farmers left parts of the field and the droppings of the harvesters so the poor could gather food.

7 THE NORTHERN KINGDOM

Two Kingdoms   In the days of Solomon, many young men were taken from their farms to be warriors in the king's army or to build the king's cities and monuments. When Solomon died, his son Rehoboam became king. The leaders of the ten tribes of the north came to Rehoboam and said, Do not take our sons as your father did. Rehoboam answered, "My father beat you with whips, but I will whip you with scorpions!" [1 Kings 12:14]

His answer split the kingdom in two. The northern tribes elected a new king, Jeroboam, and called their kingdom Israel. Rehoboam called his kingdom Judah, after the name of the largest tribe, the tribe of David and Solomon. And all along the border, there were small battles between Israel and Judah.

The Kingdom of Israel   The history of the kingdom of Israel was short and bloody. In its 200 years, it was ruled by 19 kings; eight of them died in battle or were assassinated. When one king died, many fought over the throne, sometimes killing each other.

In those days, bands of men who called themselves prophets roamed in Israel and in Judah. Some were really fortune-tellers. Some said they could speak with the dead. Some said they could find things that had been lost, heal the sick, or even bring the dead back to life. These were the false prophets.

There were others who were truly prophets. When they spoke, it was as if God were speaking. They taught the laws of God and reminded the people of Israel and Judah of the covenant between them and the Lord. When they spoke of the future, it was to warn the Israelites not to become weak by being like the other nations. The words they spoke were so powerful that even kings sometimes feared them.

The Prophet Elijah One of the most powerful of these true prophets was Elijah. He lived in the time of the evil King Ahab, who had brought idol worship back to Israel. Unafraid, Elijah appeared before Ahab in the palace. "As the Lord lives, the God of Israel whom I serve," said the prophet, "there will be no dew or rain except when I say." [1 Kings 17:1] For three years no rain fell, nor did the dew rise up in the morning. The crops withered and died; and the prayers to the gods of the Canaanites did not save the people from hunger.

At last there was a showdown. Elijah met the false prophets and the Canaanite priests on Mount Carmel, in the sight of all the people. Like a miracle, a flame came up and took the sacrifice of Elijah; but—no matter how they chanted, danced and raved—the sacrifice of the Canaanites would not catch fire. With a cry, Elijah and the Israelites fell upon the pagan priests, killing them all. Soon after, Ahab died in battle.

The Prophet Amos   From Judah came another prophet, Amos. In Bethel, in Israel, he told the people that they would soon be destroyed. God had

Elijah meets the priests of Baal on Mount Carmel.

seen that they were wicked—the rich did not help the orphan, the widow, or the poor; the merchants cheated people; and when the people offered sacrifices, they forgot God's laws and gave only their possessions, never their hearts or their minds. Now, said Amos, "Let justice roll up like the waters, and righteousness as a mighty stream" [Amos 5:24]. The words of Amos were written in a scroll, the first such book of the Prophets.

Divided Kingdoms
Mid-8th cent. B.C.E.

0 20 40 60

Byblos

LEBANON

Sidon
Damascus

Tyre

ISRAEL

The Great Sea
(Mediterranean)

JORDAN R.

Samaria

AMMON

Jerusalem

JUDAH

Gaza
PHILISTINES

MOAB

EDOM

Eilat

Israel Lost   Despite the warnings of the prophets, the people did not give up their wickedness. The end of the kingdom of Israel was near. The Assyrians under Tiglathpileser attacked the kingdom and defeated it. They took captive many of the people and sent them across the Jordan River north to Assyria. For a while, the kings of Israel still ruled; but they did all the Assyrians demanded of them.

Then one of the Israelite kings made a secret treaty with Egypt. He hoped Egypt would fight with him against Tiglathpieser's son, Shalmaneser. But when Shalmaneser heard of this, he took the Israelite king captive; and he laid siege to Samaria, the capital of Israel, encircling it. For two years the people lived safely behind the mighty walls of Samaria. But at last they surrendered; and, in 722, the last of the ten tribes of northern Israel were sent across the Jordan.

Thus the ten tribes disappeared. Some say they were married among the Assyrians and forgot God. Some say they were scattered among the other peoples taken captive by the Assyrians. Legend says they still live together somewhere beyond the magical river of Sambatyon. All that history can say is, they are lost.

An "Elijah's Cup"
for use at the Passover
Seder. This one is
inscribed with
a quotation from the
Haggadah.

ELIJAH

Like David and Solomon, Elijah found a special place
in the legends of the Jewish people. It was said that he
did not die, but was taken up to heaven in a fiery
chariot so that one day he could return to earth and
announce that the Messiah was about to come.

During the Passover Seder, we set aside a special Cup
for Elijah and open the door in the hope that the
prophet will come and tell us that the Messiah is on
the way. As Sabbath departs each week, we remember
Elijah at the close of the Havdalah ceremony, praying
that he will come soon bringing the Messiah. And,
because legend says that Elijah will be at the birth of
the Messiah, we set aside a special chair at the
circumcision of every boy, a Chair of Elijah.

Other legends say that Elijah is the famous
"wandering Jew," who walks the earth doing good
deeds and preparing for the coming of the Messiah.
And many legends in the Talmud tell of the ancient
rabbis' meeting and speaking with Elijah, hundreds of
years after his death.

8 THE KINGDOM OF JUDAH

To Jerusalem came the news of the destruction in the north. As men traded grain and fruit they paused to speak of the fall of the kingdom of Israel. Women listened to tales of the destruction of Samaria as they shopped for perfume and jewelry. For it was said by travellers that Samaria was more beautiful than even fair Jerusalem; and now it had been conquered. Surely, the people agreed, it was because golden calves had been placed at the altars of God at Bethel and Dan in the north; or perhaps because the northern tribes had worshipped the Canaanite gods.

But one prophet spoke out, saying that the Israelites were one people. God had grown angry with both north and south, and had cut off a part of the people as a warrior cuts off an enemy's hand. This prophet, Micah, warned that Judah was now in danger,

For the wound is incurable; it has reached Judah,
It has spread to the gate of my people,
To Jerusalem. [Mic. 1:9]

While the northern kingdom of Israel existed, the people of Judah had little to fear from Assyria. Now that Israel had fallen, the Assyrians were only a few miles from Jerusalem, and the king of Judah was forced to pay heavy taxes to Tiglathpileser, the Assyrian ruler.

The Altar of Ashur The weak king, Ahaz, removed the bronze altar of the Lord from the Temple and put up a huge altar to the Assyrian god, Ashur. This pleased the Assyrians, but it angered the great prophet, Isaiah. "God has spoken," said Isaiah, as he stood outside the Temple,

> *Shall I not do to Jerusalem and her images*
> *What I did to Samaria and her idols?* [Isa. 10:11]

God would surely punish the people of Judah, Isaiah said. But God would forgive them afterward, and save at least some of them. Praying on the Sabbath and at the New Moon would not help them, and offering sacrifices at the Temple would be of no use. Only one thing could help them, Isaiah said,

> *Cease to do evil; learn to do good.*
> *Devote yourselves to justice; and aid the injured.*
> [Isa. 1:16–17]

The marketplace in Jerusalem. The City of David had become a central trading city on the caravan trail between Egypt and Damascus.

In the time of war, Isaiah preached peace and friendship. The day must come, he said, when

> *Instruction shall come forth from Zion,*
> *The word of the Lord from Jerusalem . . .*
> *Nation shall not lift up sword against nation;*
> *Neither shall they study war any longer.* [Isa. 2:3–4]

Isaiah and Hezekiah   The son of Ahaz was Hezekiah. Hezekiah ordered the Temple cleansed and the idols destroyed. He set up the Lord's altar again and called the people together to celebrate Passover, a festival that had been forgotten almost completely. Then he prepared for battle against the Assyrians. Isaiah warned Hezekiah that Assyria was too mighty, but the king refused to listen to the prophet. He declared his independence.

An Assyrian artist carved this picture of a battering ram used against a walled city.

Then the Assyrian armies came into Judah. One city after another was attacked and taken. Led by their ruler, Sennacherib, the Assyrian armies encircled Jerusalem. Hezekiah surrendered, and was forced to send more of the Temple's gold and silver treasures to the Assyrian capitol, Nineveh. But Hezekiah rebelled again in 690 B.C.E.; and this time the Assyrians lost. A disease broke out in the Assyrian camp and Sennacherib was forced to turn his troops around and return to Assyria.

Hezekiah's son, Menasseh, undid all his father had done. Again, idols were worshipped in the Temple; and again taxes were paid to Assyria. And some even say that Menasseh had the prophet Isaiah put to death—for in his time, Isaiah disappeared.

Josiah and the Book of the Covenant

It was many years before a king arose in Judah to give hope to the Israelites. This was Josiah who ordered that the Temple be cleansed and all idols removed. The Bible tells how, while cleaning the Temple, one of the priests found a scroll written in the hands of Moses. This lost book—some scholars think it was Deuteronomy, the fifth book of the Torah—was read to Josiah.

Just as Assyria was growing weak and the prophet Nahum was foretelling the fall of Nineveh, Josiah called the people of Judah to come to Jerusalem to hear the holy scroll. After this reading, Josiah called on the people to accept again the covenant between God and the Israelites, just as the people had done at Mount Sinai. Then followed great rejoicing; and the spirit of the people of Judah was high. But not for long.

Josiah died in a battle against the Egyptian Pharoah Neco; and Neco placed Josiah's youngest son, Jehoiakim, on the throne. Jehoiakim, like Menasseh, undid all the good his father had done, so that—left without a strong leader—the people soon returned to the worship of idols.

Babylonian troops set
fire to the Temple.

9 THE END OF JUDAH AND THE TEMPLE

Jeremiah   At Sukkot time, in the first year of Jehoiakim's reign, Jeremiah the Prophet came to the Temple in Jerusalem. Pushing his way to the front of the crowd, he spoke out angrily:

> *Thus saith the Lord: If you do not obey Me . . . Then I will make this city a curse for all the nations of the earth.* [Jer. 26:4, 6]

Jehoiakim was angered. He hated the prophets. And hearing that another prophet, Uriah, had spoken the same words as Jeremiah, he sent his troops to capture Uriah and put the prophet to death. Even the people of Jeremiah's own city now told Jeremiah he was in danger; he should prophesy no longer.

But Jeremiah would not be silenced. He told his secretary, Baruch, to write down the words he had spoken in a scroll, and to read that scroll in Jerusalem. Jehoiakim had the scroll burned; but Baruch wrote it all down a second time, adding many new words of Jeremiah, and it became the Book of Jeremiah the Prophet.

When Jehoiakim died, the Babylonians (who had conquered the Assyrian empire and ruled in Nineveh) attacked Judah and carried Jehoiakim's son and many thousands of the people of Judah back to Babylonia as captives. Zedekiah became king of Judah.

The Fall of Jerusalem   Jeremiah warned Zedekiah to surrender to the Babylonians. It was God's plan, Jeremiah said, to punish the people of Judah. They would be taken captive and forced to serve the Babylonians for 70 years, and then they would be allowed to return to the land of Israel. But Zedekiah had Jeremiah thrown into prison. Soon after, the Babylonians encircled the city of Jerusalem.

For six months the people in Jerusalem suffered. The hunger was so great that many died. Disease began to spread. Finally, the city could hold out no longer. In 587 B.C.E., the walls fell to the Babylonian battering rams. In August, Nebuchadnezzar, the ruler of Babylon, sent his warriors to destroy the city. And this they did.

Even the Temple was not spared. The fine building that Solomon had erected, that had been at the heart of the people of Judah ever since, that had been the center of the struggle of the covenant against idolatry, now fell to the soldiers of Nebuchadnezzar. All that was in it was destroyed. Its candlesticks and pillars were broken; its altars were destroyed. Its gold and silver and bronze were carried off as the spoils of war. And the building was leveled to the ground on Tishah B'Av, the ninth day of the month of Av, 586 B.C.E. Mighty Jerusalem had fallen; the House of the Lord was no more.

The End of Judah Jeremiah was allowed to return home to Mizpah. But thousands of Israelites were taken captive and sent to Babylonia. A few years later, the people remaining in Judah revolted against Nebuchadnezzar, but the revolt was quickly put down; and some of the revolutionaries, afraid for their lives, fled to Egypt. They carried Jeremiah with them, though he was an old man now. Longing for his home in Judah, still the prophet spoke—but now he spoke words of comfort for his people.

Babylon shall become rubble,
A den for jackals,
An object of horror and hissing. [Jer. 51:37]

But the people of Judah and Israel would return to rebuild the land, said Jeremiah. And, as his words had been true before, so they would be true now. The people did return.

Many mythical animals are pictured on the Gate of Ishtar. This gate was the main entrance into Babylon.

THE TEMPLE IN RUINS

The fall of the Temple left fear and sorrow to haunt the Israelites. Perhaps God had turned away from them forever? Perhaps the covenant had at last been broken beyond repair? The sadness was so great that it was a kind of mourning, as if someone dear and precious had died.

According to tradition, the old prophet Jeremiah wrote five poems which became the Book of Lamentations. There he mourned Jerusalem,

> *How doth the city sit solitary,*
> *That was full of people!*
> *How is she become as a widow!*
> *She that was great among the nations . . .*
> *She hath none to comfort her*
> *Among all her lovers;*
> *All her friends . . . are become her enemies.* [Lam. 1:1–2]

The people believed that God had caused the destruction of Jerusalem. One legend told that the Babylonians wished to set fire to the Temple, but before they could, fire came down from heaven to destroy it. The Temple had been God's resting place on earth; and now it seemed that God was saying, "Take back My resting place, for you, O Israel, have given Me no rest."

10 THE RETURN TO JERUSALEM

The towns and cities of Judah were burned and ruined. Those people left behind began to leave. They went to Egypt, to Moab, to Edom, Ammon, and Transjordan. Some of the scattered Jews married non-Israelites, forgot their religion, and were lost like the Ten Tribes of the north. But those in Babylonia brought with them the Torah, the scrolls of the prophets, and many other writings.

Babylon as it may have looked when t[he] Judeans first saw it

Life in Babylonia   In Babylonia, the Israelites worshipped together and celebrated the holy days together. They began to speak of "building a fence around the law"; that is, adding new laws to protect the old ones from being broken. And they began to dream of a return to their homeland.

When life seemed hard in Babylonia, the Bible tells us that the people sat and wept by the waters of Babylon as they remembered their homes. And when their spirits grew weary, new prophets arose to give them cheer. One of these was Ezekiel, who had been taken captive by Nebuchadnezzar's armies in 597 B.C.E. and brought to Babylonia. His first writings had foretold the coming fall of Jerusalem, but after Jerusalem was destroyed, he wrote to comfort the people. The Temple was important, he told them, but more important still were the laws of Moses.

Another great prophet (we do not know his name, but since his teachings were added on to the scroll of Isaiah, we call him Second Isaiah) reminded the people that suffering was not always a sign of the end of life. "Comfort ye, comfort ye, My people" [Isa. 40:1], he said to them in God's name, for this suffering was only a test; and if they were true to God and followed God's laws, then God would remember them and take them out of Babylonia as they had once been taken out of Egypt

Cyrus the Great Truly it must have seemed a miracle to this Second Isaiah as he lived to see

This clay cylinder is the famous Edict of Return which allowed the Judeans to rebuild Jerusalem.

his words come true. From out of the north came a new and mighty force, the Persians. Under their ruler, King Cyrus, they conquered Babylonia. But Cyrus did not try to change the religion of the peoples he conquered, nor did he take the people captive and move them to another land. Instead, he allowed each conquered people to live in peace, to have its own religion, and its own king.

In 538 B.C.E., one year after he had conquered Babylonia, Cyprus issued an Edict of Return, a royal order allowing the people of Judah to return to Jerusalem. And he promised money from the royal treasury to help them rebuild their Temple. From the ancient family of David, he chose a king to lead the people; and a few stouthearted families began the long walk back home.

On the ruins of the first Temple, they immediately began to build a second Temple. The work was slow, and the people were forced to stop so they could fight a new enemy, the Samaritans.

Cyrus the Great on parade in his chariot.

THE VALLEY OF THE BONES

Ezekiel's most famous prophecy told of the rebirth of the nation of Israel. The people of Israel, he wrote, are like bones drying in the desert. Some might say, These bones shall never live again. But the Lord could bring the bones together, put flesh on them, breathe life into them, and make them live. In the same way, the people of Israel would live again in their homeland; and the Lord would help them rebuild their Temple.

THE SAMARITANS

In the days of trouble between Assyria and the two kingdoms of the Israelites, the Samaritans had appeared in the land. Believing that the One God was the special protector of this place, they followed the laws of Moses, and read the books of the Torah. But the scrolls of the Prophets did not interest them; and they refused to listen to the laws which had been made by the Israelites in Babylonia. When the Israelites returned to Judah, the Samaritans were angered. They wanted the land for themselves. So they began to raid the small settlement of the Israelites, to keep the Israelites from completing work on their Temple. In time, the Samaritans built their own temple on Mount Gerizim and continued to worship God in their way.

Prophets and the Temple Two prophets, Haggai and Zechariah, taught the people of Judah that the time when God would rule the earth was soon coming. The Temple was needed so that God could again be worshipped in Jerusalem. At their urging, the work on the Temple continued, and in 515 B.C.E., the building was completed and dedicated. It was smaller and less splendid than the Temple of Solomon, but its completion encouraged many Israelites to leave Babylonia and return to Jerusalem. The community grew in numbers.

But once again the Israelites in the land began to forget their religion. Many stopped observing the Sabbath; many married among the other peoples of the land. Some stopped paying taxes to the Temple.

Nehemiah and Ezra To lead this wayward community, the new king of Persia, Artaxerxes I, let one of his own attendants, an Israelite named Nehemiah go to Judea. Filled with strength and enthusiasm, Nehemiah helped the people to construct a wall around Jerusalem, to protect it from the raids of the Samaritans. And soon, he was joined by another leader from Babylonia, the famous teacher, Ezra the Scribe. Ezra brought with him the holy books, the scrolls of the Torah, many writings of the prophets, and the new laws made by the Israelites in Babylonia.

In 444 B.C.E., in the Temple court, Ezra called the people together. He read to them the books of Moses, and the Bible tells that the people wept when they heard these words. Once again they felt like one people, and they renewed their covenant with God, promising

to walk in God's law, which was given by Moses the servant of God, and to observe and do all the commandments of the Lord our Lord . . . [Neh. 10:30]

THE END OF DAYS

The prophets spoke of a time when God would end all the suffering of human beings. There would be a day of judgment—"The Day of the Lord"—and a new heaven and earth would be created. God would renew the covenant with the people Israel; and the kingdom of Israel would be restored. And some of the prophets began to speak of a time—"The End of Days"—when all human beings would worship the One God, the God of Israel.

Isaiah prophesied:

In the days to come . . .
The many peoples shall go and shall say:
"Come,
Let us go up to the Mount of the Lord,
To the House of the God of Jacob;
That He may instruct us in His ways,
And that we may walk in His paths." [Isa. 2:3]

And to this, Second Isaiah added:

For behold! I am creating
A new heaven and a new earth;

. . .
The wolf and the lamb shall graze together,
And the lion shall eat straw like the ox,
And the serpent's food shall be earth.
In all My sacred mount
Nothing evil or vile shall be done
—said the Lord. [Isa. 65:17, 25]

IN THE DAYS OF THE RABBIS

In 333 BCE, the Persian empire fell to the armies of Alexander the Great, ruler of Greece. With great speed, Alexander's armies swept through Egypt, Judah, and Syria, and conquered all the lands of the East as far as India. He was kind to the people he conquered; and the people of Judah spoke of him highly. Yet a short ten years later, Alexander was dead. His empire was carved into pieces by his generals. For a time Judea (the Greek name for Judah) was ruled by Egypt, and later by the Seleucid kings of Persia.

It was the end of a time and the beginning of a time. The period of Jewish history called the age of the Bible was over. Now began a new period—the age of the Rabbis. In this unit we shall see how the ancient Israelites became the Jewish people and carried their covenant-message across the face of the earth.

11 HELLENISM AND HASIDISM

The Diaspora   The ways of the Greeks, a culture called Hellenism, spread among the Israelites scattered throughout the vast Greek Empire. Outside of Judea, the Israelites said they were living in *Diaspora* (from the Greek word for "dispersion" or "scattering"). All through the years the Second Temple stood in Jerusalem, some Israelites would leave to seek their fortunes in the Diaspora. Many remained loyal to their religion. Many sent yearly taxes to the Temple in Jerusalem; some came to visit the Temple on the three pilgrimage festivals—Sukkot, Pesah, and Shavuot. Wherever they lived, they continued to worship the Lord. The Greeks built places of worship called *synagogues* (from the Greek word meaning "assembly" or "gathering").

In the synagogues of Alexandria, the Israelites worshipped not in Hebrew, but in Greek. Greek was the language they spoke; Hebrew was all but forgotten. Even the holy books were translated into Greek so that the Egyptian Jews could read them. Legend tells that seventy scholars were chosen to do this work of translation. Each scholar was given a copy of the Torah; and each worked separately to translate it. When at last they met to compare their work, they found to their surprise that all 70 translations were exactly the same! This Greek version was called the *Septuagint* (from the Greek word for "seventy").

It was not just Greek words such as diaspora, synagogue, and Septuagint that began to change the Israelites; it was Greek ideas as well—the culture of Hellenism. The Hellenists believed that all religions were really the same; and many of the Israelites came to believe this, too. They married gentiles; and some even stopped practicing circumcision, the sign of the covenant.

The hall of the great library at Alexandria.

In Judea   For centuries in Judea, Hebrew and Aramaic had been spoken side-by-side. Now, Hebrew was spoken far less; most people spoke Aramaic in Judea, as did the Israelites in Babylonia. Now when the Torah was read aloud, it had to be translated into Aramaic so that the people could understand it.

Yet the people loved the Temple and its worship service. They came to hear the words of Torah, and to hear the Levite choir singing; to watch the hundreds of priests offering sacrifices, and to see the High Priest in his beautiful robes. And it was hard to imagine a more glorious event than the celebration of the Day of Atonement, Yom Kippur, the one day each year on which the High Priest entered the Holy of Holies, the small room that was the heart of the Temple.

The High Priest wore this costume. Note the breastplate with its twelve jewels — one for each of the tribes of Israel.

The Great Assembly   To continue the work of "building a fence around the law," Ezra brought together an assembly of important leaders who met from time to time to discuss Torah. In a way they were like today's Congress in America and Parliament in England. They were known as the Great Assembly, and they governed the religious life of Judea. In their time they began the work of deciding which books should be added to the Torah to form the Bible. They divided the Torah into portions for each week and added portions from the Prophets for each week's reading, and they interpreted the laws of Torah as new problems were faced by the Judean community. Interpreting the Torah meant learning the Torah; so they became teachers as well, training many hundreds of students who in turn became teachers. The work they did was so important, it was said they were a part of a great chain of teaching which began with Moses and was passed down by word of mouth since the time the covenant was made at Mount Sinai.

Hellenism and Hasidism   But even in Judea, Hellenism was becoming more popular. A Greek gymnasium was built in Jerusalem and young Jews learned Greek sports there, bowing to the idols of the Greek gods. Greek clothing, hair styles, the Greek theatre, and the teachings of the Greek thinkers all became a part of the Judean way of life; and the way of life in Egypt and Babylonia, as well. Under the Greek nations a great struggle began which would last many centuries. Already among the Judeans there were some teachers who called themselves *Hasidim* ("pious" or "religious" people) and who taught that the Greek ways were *evil*.

The Hasidim pointed to the terrible problems caused by Hellenism: the cruel way in which the Greeks treated one another, slavery (once practiced by Israelites, but now thought outdated and wrong), the Greek love of war and weapons, the ignorance of the Greek common people, the way the Greeks worshipped idols and oppressed the poor, and the drunkenness so common among the Greeks. Instead, the Hasidim said, the Judeans should try to live a life of holiness and good deeds.

The common Israelites agreed with the Hasidim and did not follow the Hellenists. But many Judeans, especially the rich living in Jerusalem, followed Hellenist ways. Thus the people were split into two parties, Hasidim and Hellenists, and at times there was even warfare between them.

THE IDEA OF THE SYNAGOGUE

The synagogue was a totally new idea in the history of religion. Before, a place of worship was usually built around an altar where animal and grain sacrifices were offered to the heavens. But in the synagogue, it was not a sacrifice but a prayer that was offered. The synagogue could be placed anywhere. It might be no more than a room in which to meet; or it might be a beautiful building filled with reminders of the ancient past of the Israelite people. Although the people still believed that the Temple in Jerusalem was the central place of gathering, the synagogue idea became more and more popular and even today it is our most important institution.

The idea of the synagogue became a gift of the Israelites to all the peoples of the world. Christians took over the idea for their institution of worship, and called their synagogues churches. The people of Islam called their houses of gathering mosques. But church, mosque, or synagogue, the idea was the same.

Ruins of the synagogue at Capernaum. Enough has been restored so that we can appreciate the beauty the builders tried to achieve.

12 DANGER, REVOLT, AND ROME

Antiochus Epiphanes While the Hellenists and the Hasidim argued in Jerusalem, a king named Antiochus IV ruled over Syria and Judea. He was haughty and prideful, and he loved nothing as much as he loved himself. He took the name Antiochus Epiphanes which means "Antiochus is the living god"; but it was whispered that he should have called himself Antiochus Epimanes, "Antiochus is a madman."

Once, after a war with Egypt, Antiochus robbed the Temple in Jerusalem of all its treasures. Then, when he thought the priests were plotting against him, he sent his armies to Jerusalem to destroy the priests. It was well known that the Jews would not fight on the Sabbath, and so the armies of Antiochus waited until the sabbath to enter Jerusalem. That day they murdered many, tore down the city walls, and carried women and children off to be sold as slaves.

In 168 B.C.E., Antiochus had a statue of the Greek god Zeus placed in the Temple. Sacrifices to Zeus were made on the altar, and the blood of pigs was poured on it. Even the Hellenists were surprised by the violence of Antiochus. They had wanted Greek culture to become part of the Judean way of life, not a religion to be forced upon the Judeans against their will.

But the worst was yet to come. Antiochus now ordered that anyone who practiced the Jewish religion should be put to death. Torah scrolls were torn and burned. Keeping the Sabbath was forbidden.

Antiochus sacrificed pigs and set up idols on Jewish altars.

The Maccabees

The Judeans began to fight back. Farmers from the small towns in the hills of Judea soon united into a small army led by the priest Mattathias of the House of Hasmon. Mattathias taught the Judeans that although fighting was not normally permitted on the Sabbath, it was allowed to break the Sabbath by fighting back when attacked in order to save one's life.

When Mattathias died, his five sons led the army; and one of them, Judah, became the general. On his banners Judah wrote four letters—מ, כ, ב, י—the first letters of the words of the Bible, "Mee kamocha ba-elim adonai?" which means, "Who is like You among the mighty, O Lord?" And, because these four letters also formed the word for "hammer," Judah's soldiers called him the "Maccabee" (מַכַּבִּי); and it was said that he fought like a hammer against the enemy. Many Hasidim joined the army of Judah.

The Maccabean Revolt

At first Antitiochus paid little attention to this small army of farmers. But as one battle after another was won by the Judeans, he grew uneasy. He sent an army of forty thousand foot soldiers and seven thousand horsemen into Judea from the north. But Judah's three thousand brave farmers attacked them by night and defeated them. Antiochus sent another army from the south; and it, too, was defeated.

Now Judah and his soldiers took the city of Jerusalem. Those who were loyal to Antiochus fled to the Citadel, the last fort in the city, and remained there for several years. But the Maccabeans had captured the hill on which the Temple stood. They tore down the pagan idols, removed the stones of the Great Altar on which the pagans had sacrificed pigs, and cleansed the Temple. They put the stones of the altar in a storehouse, hoping that some day a prophet of the Lord would come and tell them what to do to make these stones holy again. And they built a new altar of large whole stones to replace the Great Altar.

On the 25th day of Kislev, exactly three years after the pagans had begun sacrificing to idols in the Temple, Judah and his priests dedicated the Temple again to the Lord and lit the golden menorah inside the Temple. For eight days they celebrated a feast with palm branches and prayer, song and sacrifice. And in time it was decided that there should be a celebration each year to remember the cleansing of the Temple and the victory of the Maccabees. And that is how the festival of Hanukkah ("Dedication") began.

Eleazar son of Mattathias was crushed when he ran beneath an elephant and stabbed it with his sword. The beast fell upon him.

THE BOOK OF DANIEL

It was in the terrible days of Antiochus' rule that the Book of Daniel—the last book to be added to the Bible—was written. In mysterious and dreamy words it tells that the end of days is near. Four great empires had rulled the earth since the time of Nebuchadnezzar and now a Messiah, a king to be appointed by God, would come to rule over all the nations and make them one. There is no need, the book taught, for the religious to take up fighting, for in the heavens the war is raging and the angels of God are fighting for God's people.

Some Hasidim believed this was true. Antiochus' laws seemed to be a test of their faith; and the way to answer was not through war, but through continuing to practice their religion. They would rely on God to save them, just as Daniel had relied on God when he fell into the hands of his enemies.

The enemies of Daniel accused him before the king, the Book of Daniel tells, and the king was forced to follow his own law and throw Daniel into a den full of lions. But the next morning, lo and behold! Daniel was still alive. Then his enemies said, "The lions were not hungry." And the King said, "Let us see if they were hungry or not"; and he threw Daniel's enemies into the lions' den, and they were destroyed. Just as God had saved Daniel, the Hasidim said, so now God would save them for their faithfulness.

niel in the den of lions.

Rome and Jerusalem   In the West, Rome conquered Macedonia where once Alexander the Great had ruled. Rome grew mighty. Judah sent messengers to the Roman senate and the two nations made a treaty of friendship. The fighting against Syria continued, however, and Judah was killed in battle. In time, Simon, Judah's brother, was made prince of Judea and the rule of the Hasmoneans (the House of Hasmon) began. Under Simon the country had a brief time of peace. The Citadel was destroyed so that no new enemy could ever hide there. Business was good, the courts judged fairly, the Temple became the center of religious life, and idolatry was outlawed in the land. Like Judah, Simon made a treaty of friendship with Rome.

But the Hasmoneans began to quarrel among themselves. Simon was murdered by his own son-in-law. A civil war began which ended when two brothers, Hyrcanus and Aristobulus, went to Rome and asked the Roman ruler Pompey to decide who should be the next king of Judea. Pompey made Hyrcanus, the weaker of the two, king in 63 B.C.E.; and soon after, Pompey visited Jerusalem. As the Judeans watched, Pompey entered the Temple where it was forbidden for pagans to go; he went even into the Holy of Holies. Surely the priests held their breath, for no one except the High Priest was allowed to enter this small room, and then only once a year.

Pompey found the room empty—the Ark had long since disappeared. Perhaps he was confused. He might have asked himself, "Do these Jews pray to nothing?" But the Judeans were not confused. Seeing that Hyrcanus, their ruler, did nothing to stop Pompey, they knew that the Hasmoneans no longer had any power at all. Jerusalem had fallen to Rome—without a battle, without a war, and without a word of surrender.

This Roman jug is very much in the style of Greece, just as Roman statues and customs were based on Greek models.

13 PHARISEES AND SADDUCEES

The Hasmonean kings came from a family of priests, so they controlled the Temple and the government. To help them rule, there were many courts in Judea, and a *Bet Din* in Jerusalem, which was both a congress and a supreme court. The priests and the well-to-do formed a political party called the Sadducees (probably named after Zadok, who had been a high priest in the time of Solomon). But most people joined another party called the Pharisees.

The Pharisees stayed apart from the government and the priesthood (the word Pharisee probably comes from the word *parosh*, which means to "separate"), though some priests joined them. They believed that the true government was the word of God as given in the Torah. But when the Pharisees said "Torah," they meant something very special. To understand what they meant, it is important to see what had happened to the Bible.

The Holy Scriptures By this time the Bible was complete. Nothing more would be added to it; nothing would be subtracted from it. First and most important, it contained the Torah, the Five Books of Moses. Then came the books of the Prophets called *Nevi'im* (the Hebrew word means "seers"). The third part was called Ketuvim ("Writings"). So the Bible was called by a name made up of the first letters of its three parts (ת , נ , and כ), the *Tanach* (תַּנַ"ךְ). In English we call it either the Bible or the Holy Scriptures ("scripture" is a Latin word meaning "writing").

Ketuvim was made up of three kinds of writings. Some are historical (Ruth, Chronicles, Ezra-Nehemiah,

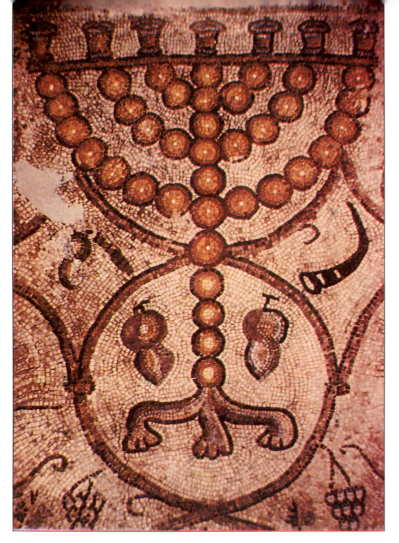

As the number of treasured Jewish books multiplied, so did the Jewish symbols used by artists. To the menorah was added the shofar and the *etrog* (citron). The *lulav* was pictured along with a Jewish symbol which has since disappeared: the incense shovel.

and Esther): they tell the story of the Jewish people up to the time of the Syrian-Greek empire. Another kind are called wisdom literature. These are books of poetry (Psalms, Song of Songs, Lamentations, Proverbs, Job, and Ecclesiastes). And one book, Daniel, is a kind of writing called apocalyptic. Many other books were written in biblical times. Most were lost, but a few—the Apocrypha, or "Hidden Books"—were collected and saved by the Christian church. By the time of the Pharisees, the first two parts of the Bible, Torah and Prophets, were complete. Most of the third part was completed by the Pharisees.

A scribe at work. For centuries, reading and writing were among the most highly prized arts of humankind.

The Written and the Oral Torahs

The Pharisees called the Bible the Written Torah or *Torah she-bich'tav*. The Sadducees believed that the Written Torah was the *only* Torah. They followed it just as it was written.

But the Pharisees believed there was a second, equally important part to Judaism, the Oral Torah or *Torah she-b'al peh*. The Oral or Spoken Torah was made up of all the teachings that had not been written down, but had passed from one generation to the next since the time of Moses. These included the words of the Scribes since the time of Ezra, of the Hasidim, and of the Pharisees themselves. For the Pharisees, the Bible was a living book, meant to be read in new ways in each generation. Of course, they believed that the laws in the Written Torah had to be followed, but not always just as they were written. For example, the Sadducees following the Written Torah said that no work could be done on the Sabbath even to save a life. The Pharisees said that the laws were meant for people to *live* by, so the Sabbath could be broken in order that a person's life might be saved.

The Sadducees kept the Sabbath so strictly that they lit no fires and allowed no fires lit before Sabbath to

A GREAT PHARISEE

One of the most famous of the Pharisee teachers was the sage Hillel. He was born of poor parents in Babylonia, and came to Judea to study Torah. He began as many students did, yet in a few short years he became the head of his own academy with hundreds of students of his own. People spoke of the School of Hillel as being one of the two most important schools of its time (the other was the School of Shammai). It was Hillel who asked the three famous questions which tell much of the religion of the Jewish people:

If I am not for myself, who will be for me?
If I am only for myself, what am I?
And if not now, when? [Avot 1:14]

When a non-Jew came and asked Hillel to explain the whole Torah while he stood on one foot, the sage did not drive him away (as Shammai had), but said:

Do not do to others what you would not have them do to you. This is the whole Torah; the rest is commentary. Now go and study. [Shab. 31a]

Hillel instructs the non-believer in the meaning of Torah.

continue burning. Sabbath eve for them was a dark time; and cold in the winter. The Pharisees taught that the Sabbath should be a time of joy. They allowed fires lit before Sabbath to burn through the next day; and started the practice of lighting extra lights just before Shabbat began—the forerunner of our Sabbath candlelighting.

The Synagogue   Through the work of the Pharisees, the synagogue became a center of Judaism. Three times a day the Pharisees led prayer services in the synagogue, just as sacrifices were offered three times a day in the Temple. So the synagogue became a House of Prayer, or *Bet Tefillah*. It was also the town meeting-place. Workers came there seeking a job, travelers came looking for a place to stay for the night, and people came in times of trouble to find help. So the synagogue became a House of Assembly, or *Bet K'nesset*. And the Pharisees took the synagogue one step further. By using it as a classroom for the people, a place where Torah was studied and explained, they turned it into a House of Study or, *Bet Midrash*. The Pharisees made the synagogues popular; and the synagogues made the Pharisees popular.

Schools   Wherever enough students could be found, the Pharisees built schools or academies. At first these were schools for adults, such as the famous schools of Hillel and Shammai. But by 70 B.C.E., there were schools for teenagers; and a hundred years later, elementary schools, too. In this way, the Pharisees taught the people Torah. They turned the people of Judea into readers and writers at a time when reading and writing were rare among the other nations of the world. In truth, they gave the Torah to the people forever.

The chain of traditio
began when Mose
received God's teach
ings on Sinai and con
tinues to this day

THE CHAIN OF TRADITION

The Pharisees saw themselves as part of a long "chain of tradition." This tradition or *mesorah* was the Oral Torah, taught by one generation of leaders to the next. Moses had received the mesorah at Sinai and had passed it on until it came to the men of the Great Assembly in the time of Ezra. So the Pharisees said,

> *Moses received the [Oral] Torah on Sinai, and handed it down to Joshua; Joshua to the elders; the elders to the prophets; the prophets to the Men of the Great Assembly.*

This saying was more than just a list of important leaders of the Jewish people. It left out one very important group—the priests.

Since the priests had joined with the Sadducees in teaching that only the Written Torah was important, the Pharisees did not think of them as a link in the great Jewish chain of tradition. And from that time to this, all Jews have agreed with the Pharisees. The Jewish way of life comes from the *whole* Torah— Written and Oral.

The Great Sea
(Mediterranean)

SYRIA

PHOENICIA

• Panias

Tiberias •
• Sepphoris

Sea of
Gallilee

JARMUK R.

TIBE PIAS

• Caesarea

JORDAN R.

Samaria •
(Sebaste)
Schechem •

JABBOK R.

N
A
B
A
T
E
A
N
S

JUDEA

Jerusalem •

Dead
Sea

ARNON R.

• Gaza

Herod's
Kingdom

about 4 B.C.E.

0   10   20   30 MI.

Ascherl

ZERED BROOK

14 HEROD, KING OF THE JEWS

Among his friends, Hyrcanus counted the wealthy Idumean, Antipater. But Antipater wanted more important friends. First, he pledged his loyalty to Pompey, who rewarded him. Then, when Antipater saw that Julius Caesar would win control of Rome in a civil war against Pompey, he sent 3,000 soldiers to help Caesar's armies in Egypt. In return, Caesar give Antipater even more power in Judea. In truth, Antipater, not Hyrcanus, now ruled over Judea.

When Antipater died in 43 B.C.E., his son Herod visited Rome, carrying with him many expensive gifts and pledges of loyalty to the new rulers, Anthony and Octavian. In return, the Roman senate declared Herod to be king of the Jews.

Herod visits the Roman Emperor Octavian.

Herod's Reign   As soon as he was on the throne, Herod ordered that 45 Hasmonean leaders be murdered. Then, to protect himself in case the people revolted against him, Herod built fortresses throughout Judea. To please his Roman friend Anthony, he called his Jerusalem fortress Antonia. But Herod was like his father: his friendship was not to be trusted.

Hearing that Octavian and Anthony were at war, and that Octavian had won an important battle at Actium in Greece, Herod met Octavian at Rhodes and promised to be loyal to the new ruler. In return, Octavian gave new lands to Herod, whose kingdom was now as large as that of King David.

Throughout the land, Herod built cities and monuments. To bring water to the inland farms, he had huge aqueducts and waterworks made. Using tax money and money from the sale of copper that he mined in Cyprus, he built a new seaport that he called Caesara in honor of Octavian, the Caesar of Rome. He rebuilt the

HEROD'S FIGHT FOR POWER

It was one thing to be named king of the Jews by the Roman senate; and another actually to become king. In Jerusalem, Antigonus of the House of the Hasmoneans ruled. Even though he was a weak ruler, the people liked him because he was a Hasmonean and because he was truly a Jew.

Herod was a half-Jew. Idumea (the ancient land of Edom) had been converted to Judaism by conquest and by force when Antigonus' great-grandfather, John Hyrcanus, made it a part of Judea. And, although tens of thousands of Idumeans became Jews, few followed the Jewish religion. Thus, Antipater married a non-Jewish wife, Cypros, who became Herod's mother; and being the child of a Jew and a non-Jew, Herod was only a half-Jew.

To make himself more popular among the Jews, Herod chose as his second wife a Hasmonean princess named Mariamne, the niece of Antigonus. With Hasmoneans on both sides of the struggle for the throne of Judea, the people were divided, and Herod was able to defeat Antigonus in 37 B.C.E. All his life, Herod lived in fear that the people would revolt against him; some scholars believe that it was this fear that finally drove him to madness and murder.

This tablet, found at Tel Mevorakh, indicates that the Tenth Roman Legion was stationed here.

Herod built Herodium as a desert fortress. It is said that Herod was buried on top of this mountain in a full-sized golden coffin. Archaeologists have looked, but the tomb of Herod has yet to be found.

ancient city of Samaria, naming it, too, after Octavian; and built two new fortresses on the edge of the desert, calling each after himself, Herodium. Then Herod strengthened the old fortress on the Dead Sea, built atop the mountain of Masada; and he built there a palace as grand as his palace in Jerusalem.

Herod and the Temple   To please the Jews and to impress the Romans, Herod ordered that the Temple be made more beautiful. The small building completed in the time of Ezra and Nehemiah was now enlarged and made a two-story brick structure. The priests were paid to rebuild the Holy of Holies, which no non-Jew or non-priest was allowed to touch; and other Judeans built the many courts around the Temple. Finally, the whole hilltop on which the Temple stood was surrounded by a wall. All that remains today is a part of that wall, the Western Wall, and it is still thought to be the holiest of all Jewish places.

True, the Jews were pleased when Herod made the Temple so grand, but they were dismayed when the king then placed a Roman eagle, like an idol, on the Temple gate. And they felt betrayed when they saw that Herod built a temple in Samaria for the worship of the Roman

Emperor. Nor were they happy when Herod built a Roman theater and a hippodrome for horse and chariot races in Jerusalem; and brought back the athletic games such as those that had been held in the Greek gymnasium.

Coin issued in the time of Herod.

Herod and the Jews   While Hillel was teaching that fair treatment of others was the cornerstone of Judaism, and Shammai was teaching that people should greet one another in kindness, Herod was murdering his family. The king had married ten wives; he had many children. Of all his wives, he loved Mariamne the best; and of all his sons, he loved her two boys the best. Yet he murdered Mariamne to please his mother; and he murdered her two sons to please his daughter, Salome. Once he asked Octavian for permission to put another son to death for plotting against him. Octavian agreed, saying, "It is better to be Herod's pig than his son."

It is no wonder that the Pharisees wanted no part of the government. The Sanhedrin, which had grown out of the old Bet Din of the Hasmoneans, had no real power any longer; but only agreed to whatever Herod said. Leaving government to the Sadducees and others, the Pharisees studied and taught, prayed three times a day, and settled the arguments that the people brought to them. More and more the people trusted the Pharisees and hated the king and his government.

When the king lay ill and dying, the people of Jerusalem rioted and tore down the eagle from the Temple gate. Even at the door of death, Herod remained fierce and cruel. He commanded that the rioters and their leaders be burned to death. There were few to mourn Herod's passing in 4 B.C.E.—few among the people, and few among his family.

The Sanhedrin meets.

THE SANHEDRIN

For many years in the time of the Second Temple, the Great Assembly met to speak of religious matters. Legend says that there were 120 sages in the Great Assembly, and we know that they had long discussions which shaped Jewish prayer and the prayer services for all time to come.

Under the Pharisees a new assembly arose, called the Sanhedrin. Seventy-one rabbis and scholars met together in one of the large halls of the Temple. At the head of the Sanhedrin sat the *Nasi* (from the Hebrew word for "prince") who was usually from the family of Hillel. And beside the Nasi sat the *Av Bet Din* (Hebrew for "the Father of the Court of Justice"). So the Sanhedrin met for two reasons. First, it met to discuss matters of religion and Jewish law. And, second, it met as the Supreme Court of the Jewish people.

e "dagger men" struck fear in the holy
y of Jerusalem. Not only Romans were
aid, but the many Jews who helped
>me and befriended the Romans were
rified.

15 THE LAST DAYS OF JUDEA

Herod's children divided up the country, but in the year 6 C.E. the Romans sent governors called *pro-curators*, tax collectors called *publicans*, and *legions* of soldiers. Judea was now officially ruled by Rome. The procurators changed often. None of them was interested in governing Judea; all were interested in stealing what they could.

Everywhere the Jews spoke of rebellion against Rome. In the north, the Galilee, a new party was formed called the Zealots. They vowed to fight Rome to the death. Under their cloaks they carried small knives which they used to stab their enemies—Romans, and Jews who helped Rome—and for this reason they were called *Sicarii* ("dagger men"). Romans, and most Jews, thought of the Zealots as terrorists.

Crucifixion To stop the riots in Jerusalem and the rebellion in the north, the procurators used cruelty and force. Quintillus Varus, an early procurator, crucified two thousand Judeans for rioting. They were hung on two thousand wooden crosses hammered upright into the ground, and left to die of thirst, hunger, or the hot Judean sun. The Romans were not the first to use crucifixion as a punishment. Antiochus IV, fighting against the Hasmoneans, had crucified Judeans; and before the Greeks, the Persians had used this torture to the death. But the Romans used it regularly in Judea, hoping the Jews would come to fear the power of Rome. Instead, the Judeans grew angrier; they rioted more; and more of them were crucified.

Pilate and Jesus of Nazareth For a long ten years, from 26 to 36 C.E., Pontius Pilate held the office of procurator. Before, people had court trials before being put to death, but Pilate did away with the trials. Throughout the Galilee and in Jerusalem, he crucified Judean rebels and leaders. He angered the Jews by trying to use Temple money to build a Roman aqueduct; and by allowing his legions to bring their imperial images (idols) into Jerusalem. In the end, Rome heard of his evil and called him back from Judea.

Among the rebels and leaders Pilate crucified was Jesus of Nazareth. In the Galilee, Jesus had been a popular teacher. He may have been a Pharisee, for many of his ideas were also teachings of the Pharisees. But Jesus believed that the world was about to end; and that, in these times, the law was not as important as just loving your neighbor. The Pharisees thought this belief would never lead to action. Without the law, what could "loving your neighbor" really mean? For example, you can love orphans without feeding them; but through the law to feed and help orphans you truly learn what loving orphans means. For the Pharisees, law and love were two sides of one coin; one without the other had no meaning.

Jesus came to Jerusalem one Passover and said that he was the messiah for whom the Jews had been praying. His followers spread this message among the many who had come to visit the Temple, and soon the priests heard of it. Afraid that he would cause riots, the priests handed Jesus to Pilate. Pilate, who hated and feared all rebels, was only too glad to crucify Jesus.

A coin from the first century. The words around the outside are "a shekel of Israel." Today the Israel government calls its basic coin a "shekel."

The War With Rome　Among the last procurators was Gessius Florus, a man whose cruelty was greater even than Pilate's. Hoping to enrich himself, Florus plotted to force the Jews to rebel against Rome. When they did, he hoped to kill them, take what was left of their money, and rob the Temple's treasures. But when the Jews did rebel in 66 C.E., they killed so

CHRISTIANITY

Jesus might have been forgotten like the thousands of other Jews who were crucified if it had not been for his follower, Paul. Seeing that his fellow Jews refused to believe that Jesus was the messiah, Paul began preaching a new religion. He traveled through the Roman empire teaching that Jesus was not really dead. He was ruling in the heavens, said Paul, ready to help anyone who believed in him. He was a special son of God, said Paul, calling Jesus the *Christ* (Greek for "messiah"). Thus Paul spread Christianity.

Paul was able to make many converts among the pagans. Life was so hard that people believed true happiness would only come in heaven after they died. But the Jews believed strongly in life, and said that happiness had to be found in living. As the Torah taught:

> *. . . I have set before you life and death, the blessing and the curse, therefore choose life, that you may live, you and your children . . .* [Deut. 30:19]

To the Jews any true messiah would rule the nations of this world, the living world; not nations in a world of the dead. So the new religion of Christianity made little sense to them.

This angered the early Christians, who wanted all Jews to join them; and as time went on they began to teach that Pilate had been a kind man and the Pharisees had forced poor Pilate to crucify Jesus. Sixteen hundred years would pass before the Church finally said that this was not true. And in those sixteen centuries, the Jews would suffer time and again because the Church called them "Christ-killers."

many Romans that even Florus was amazed. The Roman emperor Nero sent his best general, Vespasian, to lead the Roman legions against the Jews. In 67, Vespasian forced the Jewish army of the Galilee and its commander, Josephus, to surrender. Josephus, believing that the end for the Jews was near, befriended Vespasian, and began writing a history of the war.

Having conquered the Galilee, Vespasian slowly marched to Jerusalem where the Sadducees, the Pharisees, the Zealots, and the remaining Jewish army had gathered. In 69, after the death of Nero, Vespasian became emperor of Rome, leaving his son Titus to continue the war in Judea. Titus and his legions surrounded Jerusalem and waited. Inside the walls, the people began to die of hunger. Outside, the Romans piled up dirt to make ramps and pushed their battering rams up the ramps to the walls. Finally, in the Hebrew month of Av, 70, the battering rams crashed heavily on the walls. But the walls were too strong, so Titus had the gates of the Temple area burned, and fire consumed the gates and the Temple, too. The Roman soldiers rushed through the

The Arch of Titus in Rome shows the Roman armies carrying off the menorah and the gold and silver utensils used in the Temple.

An archaeologist's model of the Second Temple in the time of Herod (left). Most of the people of Jerusalem lived in the crowded houses along the Ofel Valley where David's original city had been. This photo of the model (below) is the view looking up from the valley to the Temple mount.

opening and fell upon the women, children, and old men who had hidden in the Temple courts, killing them without mercy. Then Titus burned the upper and the lower cities of Jerusalem, leaving only one outer wall of the Temple and three towers of Herod's palace so that all could see the glory that the Romans had destroyed.

Masada The Zealots fled from Jerusalem to the desert fortress of Masada by the Dead Sea. For three years, they farmed the land atop the mountain, as the Roman armies encircled them far below. The Romans built a ramp of dirt and garbage from the bottom of the valley to the mountaintop, and led their battering rams to the fortress walls. The fighting was fierce. The Jews shot arrows from the tops of the walls, poured burning oil on the Roman soldiers below, and showered the Romans with rocks. But nothing would stop the battering rams.

Then, just as the walls were falling, the fighting from above stopped. The battering ram broke through the last foot of stone, and the Romans rushed into the fortress, swords drawn, ready for revenge. But the Zealots had saved the last victory for themselves. Only silent bodies were left atop Masada. Instead of becoming Roman slaves, the Zealot men had chosen to kill their own wives and children, and then to kill themselves.

The war against Rome lasted seven years. The Jews had been defeated; the Temple had been destroyed. The land belonged to Rome; many Judeans were taken captive to be sold as slaves. To erase the memory of the Jews, the Romans renamed the land Palestine (after the Philistines). It would be 1,900 years before a Jewish state arose again in the land. But the Romans had failed to destroy Torah, and because of that the Jewish people would live longer than the empire that defeated them.

One of the many storehouses that Herod's engineers built on top of Massada. In Herod's days, these were kept well-stocked with grain.

The Great Sea

N
W   E
S

Qumran Caves

Jerusalem ●

Herodium ●

Dead

● Gaza

Sea

Masada ▣

Beersheba ●

Masada

MASSADA. On this desert mountaintop, Herod built a grand three-tiered palace, a full Roman bath, huge water cisterns, warehouses for grains and other food, soldiers' barracks, and a small town.

16 OLD WAYS AND NEW

Jewish scholars believe that by the time the Temple was destroyed in 70 C.E., the priests and their sacrifices were no longer at the center of the Jewish way of life. If the Temple sacrifices had been important, they say, surely the Jews living outside the Holy Land would have sent warriors, weapons, or money to help the Judeans stop the Roman armies. Since we know it took the Romans three years to capture Jerusalem, there would have been time enough for help to come from the Diaspora. But there was no help. Why?

Philo and the Jews of Egypt In Egypt, especially in the large busy city of Alexandria, there were new ideas about the meaning of being Jewish, and many of these ideas came from the work of one man, Philo. He lived from 20 B.C.E. to 45 C.E.; and he studied both Greek and Jewish writings, teaching that both nations really had the same thoughts and beliefs.

For example, in Greece the teachers called the Stoics said that the old Greek myths were not stories about real gods and goddesses, but tales to teach people important lessons. Likewise, Philo said the Bible was made up of stories less about real people than about important ideas. So the story of the burning bush teaches us that God's ways cannot always be understood by human beings, just as Moses could not understand how a bush could burn and not be destroyed by flames.

The Greek philosopher, Plato, had said that our world is not the true world, for in the true world Good rules; but though we try to reach the Good in this world, we always fall short of it. Philo said that what the Greeks called the "Good" was called "God" by the Jews. Like the Good, God is above the world and separate from it; and though we may reach toward God with our bodies in this world, only our spirits can truly come close to God.

The Greek Jews of Egypt came to believe that sacrifices, like those of the Temple in Jerusalem, were less important than keeping the laws with a good heart. Most Egyptian Jews had never seen the Temple (the Jews of Leontopolis, in Egypt, had built their own "temple"), but they had read the popular writings of Philo; and they felt good about their new Jewish way of life built on the synagogue and deeds of lovingkindness.

The Jews of Babylonia Philo's writings did not reach the Jews of Babylonia, yet they also had built a new Jewish way of life around the synagogue. True, they were angered when they heard the news that the Temple in Jerusalem had been destroyed. After all, the Temple was a Jewish holy place—the most impor-

The Dead Sea Scrolls were discovered in 1947. Most importantly, they show that the versions of the Bible we have today are virtually the same as they were in the first century.

Reconstructing the homes of the Dead Sea people show that they lived very simply, true to their belief that the world was about to end and purity was essential.

tant of all Jewish holy places. But they read the words of the Jewish historian Josephus who told them that it was not Rome's fault that the Temple was destroyed, for the Jews of Judea had rebelled against Rome, and the Romans had little choice. Later the Babylonian Jews would rise against Rome, not because of the destruction of the Temple, but because the Roman emperor Trajan brought his armies to Babylonia. To the Babylonian Jews the loss of the Temple was a tragedy like the loss of a distant uncle, but not like the loss of a brother or sister.

The People of the Dead Sea   The Zealots thought that God would send a warrior to be the messiah. This fierce warrior-messiah would lead them to

THE DEAD SEA SCROLLS

Until 1947 we knew very little about the Essenes. But in that year, an Arab shepherd found seven scrolls in a cave near the Dead Sea; and four of them were sold to Professor Eliezer Sukenik of Israel. Looking at the first one, Sukenik grew very excited, for he knew that these scrolls were the most important archaeological discovery of modern times. Surely there were more scrolls in other nearby caves, yet the work of finding them would have to wait, for just at that moment the Jews of modern Israel were fighting for their lives against seven Arab nations. Only when the Israeli War of Independence was over in 1949 did archaeologists begin searching the caves near Qumran on the Dead Sea; and many other scrolls were discovered there.

Among these ancient scrolls are the oldest copies of every book of the Bible except the book of Esther; copies of many books which we knew were written in ancient times, but which we thought were lost forever—like the Book of Jubilees; and copies of books which tell of the life lived by the peoples of the Dead Sea community.

The Dead Sea Scrolls, among other things, proved once and for all that the Bible we study today is almost exactly the same as that studied by the sages of old, the words we read are the same words that were read by Hillel and Shammai and their many students and followers.

Jars in which the Dead Sea Scrolls were found. The scrolls were protected through the years both by the clay of the jars and by the dry heat of the Judean desert.

The mountains near the Dead Sea. The caves of Qumran in which scrolls were found can be seen as very dark spots on the mountainside.

victory over the Romans, and would help them destroy the false priests in the Temple. Like many of the Galileans, the Zealots believed that the world was about to end, so the messiah would soon come to punish Rome for its evil against God's chosen people. The Zealots carried weapons, killed Romans and Jews who aided Romans, and followed many leaders whom they called "messiahs."

But another group of Jews believed that God would send not only a warrior-messiah, but bands of heavenly soldiers to defeat Rome and remove the false priests from the Temple. This group was called the Essenes. Like the Zealots, the Essenes believed that the world was about to end; and a new world would soon begin. So they moved away from Jerusalem to become farmers and shepherds at Qumran in the hills near Ein Gedi on the Dead Sea, to study the holy books, and to plan for their parts as the priests in the new world to come. There would soon be a final war, one of their writings tells, and the world's people would be divided into two camps: the "sons of light" and the "sons of darkness."

This idea was very much like a Persian religion called Zoroastrianism, which later taught that there are two gods at war over the world, one the god of light, the other of darkness. But, being Jews, the Qumran people believed in only the One God, who would send the "prince of light," the warrior-messiah, against the "angel of darkness." And the "prince of light" would triumph; and the people of Qumran, the Essenes, would again be God's chosen priests.

Some of the Dead Sea peoples may have believed in two messiahs, for another writing tells that one messiah would come to be king over the Jews, while a second messiah would be the new High Priest. In any case, when the Qumran people saw that the Romans were near, they sealed up their precious holy books in pottery jars or wrapped these scrolls in linen and hid them in the caves nearby, where they lay for centuries waiting for the Jews to return to the land of Israel to find this most wondrous of all buried treasures.

Along with the scrolls and the jars, inkwells were found. These specially designed clay pots were tools of the trade for ancient scribes.

The Pharisees　　Most of the people believed as the Pharisees did, that the Temple sacrifices were not being offered correctly. The Pharisees, too, turned away from the Temple before it was destroyed. Like the Jews of Babylonia and Egypt, they lived lives centered on the synogogue and study. Their plan was not one of war, but one of creating a new Jewish life.

In these harsh times, the Pharisees held fast to the Torah and believed the biblical commandment, "You shall be a kingdom of priests and a holy people" [Exod. 19:6]. While some Jews believed that the laws of purity were only for the priests in the Temple to follow, the Pharisees taught that these laws were for every Jew to follow. The Pharisees did not turn their backs on the Temple entirely because they believed that it was holy to God. As long as it stood in Jerusalem, the Pharisees sent sacrifices to the priests there; but when the Temple was destroyed, they did not believe that Judaism had come to an end or that the world would soon come to an end.

17 THE WORK OF THE RABBIS

It was said that Hillel had eighty students. The youngest was Yohanan ben Zakkai. As Hillel lay dying, his many students gathered to hear his last words, but Yohanan did not feel important enough to come near. Then Hillel asked, "Where is Yohanan?" The students said, "Outside." And Hillel said, "Bring him near, for the youngest of you is the father of wisdom and the father of the future."

Hillel calls for Yohanan, his
youngest student.

The Father of Wisdom   The School
of Hillel passed from Hillel's son to his grandson to his
great-grandson. Teaching had become so important to
the Pharisees that these sages were later called the *Tannaim* (from the Aramaic word *tanna*, meaning
"teacher"). To teach the laws and customs of Judaism,
these rabbis wove together verses from the Bible and
stories and legends in what was known as *Midrash* or
"Explanations." Like many other Pharisees, Yohanan
went to the Galilee to become a teacher.

In the Galilee he likely met many of the fierce beliefs
of the Zealots for the first time. He saw that the people
there paid more attention to warriors than teachers; and
that they followed many a false warrior-messiah. Later
he taught his students that it was more important to
plant a seedling tree than to run to greet a messiah. In the
Galilee he found only one true student, Hanina ben
Dosa, and so he returned to Jerusalem, disappointed with
the Jews of the north.

It was in Jerusalem that Yohanan became a true
leader of the Pharisees. He argued against the Temple
priests and the Sadducees. God, said Yohanan, was interested in good actions more than in sacrifices on the
Temple altar. Peace, he said, was more important than
victory over Rome. Thus his words, like the words of the
ancient prophets before the First Temple was destroyed,
were displeasing to the priests.

When the Roman armies came and encircled
Jerusalem, Yohanan was trapped inside. But soon, he
made a plan to escape. Tradition said that the ground of
the Holy Land was holy, and so the dead of Jerusalem
were buried without any coffin. Pretending to be dead,
Yohanan had his students carry his limp body outside the
walls to the cemetery. Once past the gates, he and his
students went to the Roman camp and were taken to see
the Roman general, Vespasian.

Roman coin issued to celebrate the conquest of Judea. The palm tree in the center is the symbol of the land of Israel. Judea is seen as a woman in chains and crying, as Rome in the form of a soldier of the legion looks on.

Yohanan greeted the Roman general, saying, "Hail to thee, Emperor of Rome." Vespasian said, "I am no emperor." But Yohanan replied, "Soon you will be." The general ordered that Yohanan stay in the camp. Soon word reached Vespasian that Nero had died and Vespasian had indeed been made Emperor of Rome. Now the general called Yohanan and asked what the sage wished as a favor. In truth, Yohanan might have wished to save the Temple, but he knew that Vespasian would not grant him such a wish, so he asked instead to save the rabbis. He wanted Vespasian to allow a school to be built in Yavneh where the Pharisees could meet, pray, and study Torah. To this, Vespasian agreed.

But to the Jews still trapped within the walls of Jerusalem, encircled by the Roman legions, Yohanan seemed little more than a traitor.

The Father of the Future   But Yohanan was no traitor. He had a vision of a new way of life for the Jews, a life of religion and study and not of national independence, a life of Torah. When Yohanan heard that Jerusalem was destroyed and the Temple was in flames, he and his students tore their clothing, wept, and cried in mourning.

Once, when he and his student Rabbi Joshua were walking past the ruins of the Temple, Joshua began to weep.

> *"Woe unto us," Joshua cried, "that this place where offerings were made to God so that the sins of Israel would be forgiven, is now destroyed."*
>
> *"My son," said Yohanan to him, "be not grieved. We have another way of asking God to forgive our sins. And what is it? It is deeds of lovingkindness . . ."*
> *[ARNa 4; ARNb 7]*

Together with other Pharisees and his own students, Yohanan set up a new Sanhedrin as a supreme court for the Jews. The Romans now ruled the land, but the Sanhedrin began to make laws to rule the religious life of the people. The shofar was heard at Yavneh as it had been at the Temple; and the priestly blessing was given there after the Temple was destroyed.

Most of all, Yohanan urged his students to pray and study, to act kindly to others, and to see the world with an eye to what is good in it. Probably he did not know, even to his dying day, whether he had been right in leaving Jerusalem. Probably he did not know whether he had helped to save Judaism, or whether he had created a court of fools that soon no one would recall. Yet, as Hillel had promised, history tells us that Yohanan was the "father of wisdom and the father of the future."

THE SANHEDRIN AT YAVNEH

Gamaliel II became the head of the Sanhedrin at Yavneh after the death of Yohanan ben Zakkai. Many of the things we take for granted about our Jewish way of life today were begun or set down by this Sanhedrin. The basic prayer service, the laws of celebrating feasts and fasts, the weekly reading of the Torah and Prophets—these began in Yavneh. Schools were set up throughout the land to teach Torah. The Sanhedrin judged arguments between Jews, making sure that all followed the ways of Torah in business, in charity, and in righteousness. As time passed, the Jews slowly grew to trust the rabbis of Yavneh; and the synagogues and the houses of study became as important in Judea as they had been in the Diaspora.

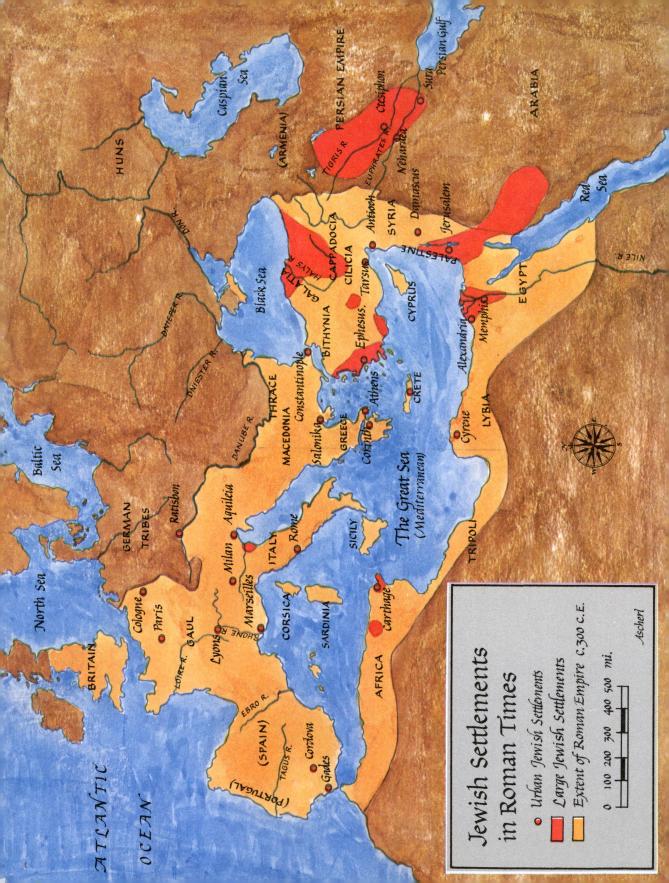

HUNS

Caspian Sea

(ARMENIA)

PERSIAN EMPIRE

Persian Gulf

Sura

Ctesiphon

TIGRIS R.

EUPHRATES R.

Nehardea

ARABIA

DNIEPER R.

DNIESTER R.

DNIESTER R.

Black Sea

GALATIA

HALYS R.

CAPPADOCIA

CILICIA

Tarsus

Antioch

SYRIA

Damascus

Jerusalem

PALESTINE

Red Sea

NILE R.

BITHYNIA

Ephesus

CYPRUS

Alexandria

Memphis

EGYPT

THRACE

Constantinople

MACEDONIA

Salonika

GREECE

Corinth

Athens

CRETE

Cyrene

LYBIA

The Great Sea
(Mediterranean)

Baltic Sea

GERMAN TRIBES

Ratisbon

Aquileia

Milan

Rome

ITALY

SICILY

TRIPOLI

North Sea

BRITAIN

Cologne

Paris

GAUL

Lyons

LOIRE R.

RHONE R.

Marseilles

CORSICA

SARDINIA

Carthage

AFRICA

ATLANTIC OCEAN

DANUBE R.

EBRO R.

(SPAIN)

TAGUS R.

Cordova

Gades

(PORTUGAL)

DON R.

Jewish Settlements
in Roman Times

- ● Urban Jewish Settlements
- ■ Large Jewish Settlements
- ▨ Extent of Roman Empire c. 300 C.E.

0 100 200 300 400 500 mi.

Ascher

18 BAR KOCHBA'S REBELLION

In 114 C.E., Trajan, the emperor of Rome, invaded the Persian Empire in Babylonia. As one, the Jews living in the Roman lands of Egypt and Cyprus decided this was the moment to make war against Rome from within. There were two reasons why the Roman Jews were willing to fight now. One was the belief that Rome was weakened by the many wars it was waging on its eastern fronts—after all, many of the Roman legions were fighting along distant borders and there were few legions in the towns and cities of Egypt and Cyprus.

The other reason that the Jews felt the time for fighting Rome was right was their belief that God would help them. After the destruction of the Temple, many Zealots had fled to Egypt and Babylonia. There they spread their teaching that the end of the world was near, and that God would soon send a warrior-messiah to help the Jews overthrow Rome.

In the end, no warrior-messiah came to aid the Jews. The Persian armies forced Rome to retreat from Babylonia; but the Romans crushed the Jewish rebellion with the full might of their armies. True, thousands of Roman soldiers were killed by the Jews. But the price was too high. The great Jewish community of Alexandria was defeated and soon disappeared forever, the Jews were cleared from the island of Cyprus and never again allowed to return, and the Jews of Babylonia who still remained within reach of the Roman armies were punished severely.

The Warrior-Messiah Comes   Still, the rebellion of 114–115 C.E. gave new hope to the Jews still living in Judea. Despite the great defeat the Jews had suffered in the Diaspora, their courage gave courage to the Judeans. Peace hung by a thin thread as Trajan died in 117; and Hadrian, the new emperor, suddenly cut that thread. Hadrian sent out an order forbidding the Jews to practice circumcision. Now even the Pharisees were en-

This is a fragment of a letter written by Bar Kochba in the second century.

raged, for circumcision was one of the most important of all Jewish commandments.

At this very moment, a leader came forward whose name was Simon bar Coziba. Around him, he gathered an army of the strongest and the mightiest of the young men of Judea. It was said that each man who came to him was tested personally by Simon to see that he had the courage and strength necessary to join the army. With Simon to lead them, the thrill of war echoed even in the teachings of the Pharisees.

RABBI AKIBA'S MESSIAH

The rebellion began while Akiba ben Joseph was head of the Sanhedrin at Yavneh. Akiba had begun his studies late in life, but was known far and wide as a great student of Torah. In making new laws, he based them not only on the teachings of the Torah, but on the letters which made up each word of the Torah. He arranged all the many sayings of the rabbis into simple categories so that students could easily remember them. And he was known to be a fair man; kind to the poor, the widow, and the orphan.

When Akiba met Simon bar Coziba, he was convinced that at last God had truly sent a messiah. Some of the rabbis, remembering the words of Yohanan, protested that Simon was just another of the many false warrior-messiahs, but Akiba paid them no heed. He renamed the warrior, Simon bar Kochba, "Simon the Son of the Star," and he went up and down the countryside calling on all Jews to unite behind Bar Kochba to fight against Rome.

The Bar Kochba Rebellion   In 132, the war against Rome began. Jews hid in forts, caves, and passageways, darting out to attack the Roman soldiers, then returning to their hiding places. Jerusalem was soon recaptured; and coins were issued by the followers of Bar Coziba (now called Bar Kochba) proclaiming the liberation of the Jews. An altar was set up in Jerusalem; and some began to speak of rebuilding the Temple.

But Hadrian moved his best general from Britain to Palestine, and sent his armies against the Jewish rebels. Slowly the tide turned against Bar Kochba's armies. Jerusalem again fell to Rome. To crush the hopes of the Jews forever, the Romans built a new city on the ruins of Jerusalem, and called it *Aelia Capitolina*. On the hilltop

Plotting a new revolt against Rome.

where the Jewish Temples had stood, the Romans built a temple to their god Jupiter. And no Jew was allowed to enter Aelia Capitolina.

The last of Bar Kochba's warriors gathered in the strong desert fortress of Betar, near Jerusalem. They fought on against Rome for one more year, but in 135 Betar was taken and Bar Kochba was killed. No bloodier war was ever fought by the Jewish people; as many as half a million Jews died in the savage fighting. Many more died of hunger once the war was over. Some died in shipwrecks as the Romans sent them to Egypt or Gaza. Captured Jews were sold as slaves. A thousand villages were in ruins and fifty walled fortresses had fallen. For the first time, the Jews were a minority in their own land.

kiba continued to teach his students from
ison. They gathered below the windows
stening to his words.

19 DEFEAT AND VICTORY

Hadrian and the Rabbis Now Hadrian decided to end the Jewish faith forever. Throughout the land of Israel he outlawed the study of Torah, the ordaining of new rabbis, and the observance of Shabbat. Yet the rabbis continued to do all these things. Akiba was arrested and thrown in jail for teaching the Torah. But while he was in jail, his student Meir would come and sit beneath the window of his jail cell and write down Akiba's teachings. Enraged, Hadrian had Akiba tortured to death. To the very end, Akiba continued to pray and teach.

The Romans hunted down the rabbis one by one; and tortured those they found. Ten great leaders were cruelly put to death. The last of them, seeing that he was about to be captured, called together all of Akiba's best students and ordained them as new rabbis. Then he ordered them to flee for their lives so that they could carry on the teaching of Torah.

After the Bar Kochba rebellion, the bans were slowly lifted. Torah could again be taught, circumcision practiced, rabbis ordained, Shabbat observed. The school of Yavneh was gone, but the rabbis who had escaped Roman torture gathered together at Usha. Simon the son of Gamaliel was made the head of the Sanhedrin; but the greatest teacher was Meir, the student of Akiba. Meir continued the work of Akiba by collecting sayings of the rabbis and arranging them as Akiba had done. It was said that his judgments were as clear as those of his teacher; and it was said that his wife Beruriah, whose teachings also appear among those of the rabbis, was one of the greatest scholars of the time.

Rabbi Judah There were two names for the head of the Sanhedrin. The Romans called him a *Patriarch*. The Jews called him a *Nasi* or "Prince."

In 170, the son of Simon became the Patriarch at Usha. His name was Judah, but he was known for all times as Judah ha-Nasi, "Judah the Prince." Judah was the last of the Tannaim, the Teachers. He was wealthy, learned, and generous. He was loved by all his colleagues; and he loved them all. Many of them called him a *tzaddik* or "saint." He was said to be a close friend of a Roman emperor (perhaps Marcus Aurelius, who was, like Judah, a man of learning and kindness, and who lived at about this time).

Judah's great work was the final collection of laws and sayings called the *Mishnah* ("Repetition"). All the scholars of his day helped him to bring together this book; and they used the collection made by Akiba and Meir as the core of it.

The Mishnah The Mishnah is made up of six volumes called Orders—*Seeds* (laws of farming and prayer); *Seasons* (laws of observing Shabbat and holy days); *Women* (laws of marriage, divorce, and vows); *Damages* (laws of business, ethics, and criminal laws); *Holy Things* (the laws of sacrifice in the Temple, and the laws of Temple worship); and *Purities* (laws of cleanliness and holiness). Each Order is divided into Tractates; and each Tractate is divided into chapters and paragraphs. The Mishnah speaks of every kind of human action, giving teachings of 148 rabbis who are mentioned by name in its pages.

The Jews had suffered a great defeat at the hands of the Romans. Yet they had gained a great victory through their study and work. Much of the Oral or Spoken Torah was now set down in writing for all to study. More work lay ahead and more of the Oral Torah still had to be written down, but this much was clear: the religion of the Jewish people and its way of life would survive.

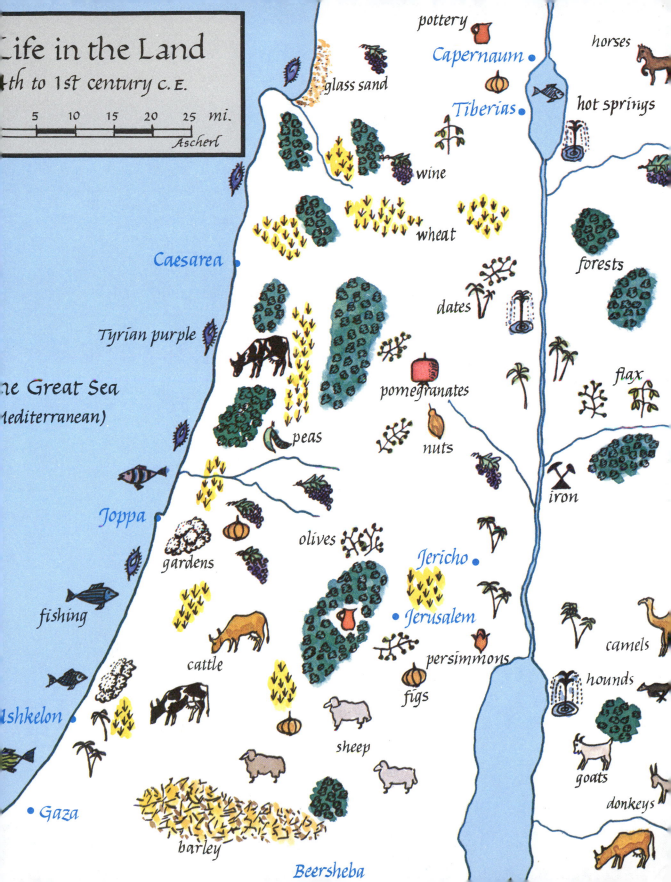

Life in the Land
4th to 1st century C.E.

5 10 15 20 25 mi.

Ascherl

pottery

Capernaum

horses

glass sand

Tiberias

hot springs

wine

wheat

Caesarea

dates

forests

Tyrian purple

flax

The Great Sea
(Mediterranean)

pomegranates

nuts

peas

iron

Joppa

gardens

olives

Jericho

fishing

Jerusalem

cattle

persimmons

camels

figs

hounds

Ashkelon

sheep

goats

Gaza

barley

donkeys

Beersheba

PIRKE AVOT

Much of Mishnah is made up of laws and cases, rules for living the life of Torah. Reading it is a little like going to school to become a lawyer. But in the Order of *Nezikin* (Damages) there is one small tractate called *Pirke Avot*, "The Sayings of the Fathers," made up of the great moral teachings of sixty of the Tannaim. In a way, Pirke Avot sums up much of the ethical concerns, the folklore and outlook, the law, legend, and principles of Mishnah. In its five short chapters there is the feeling of meeting the sages face to face. Here are a few of its sayings:

> *Ben Zoma said: Who is wise? The person who learns from all; as it is said, 'From all my teachers I have taken wisdom.'*

> *Rabbi Tarphon said: The day is short, and the work is great, the laborers are slow, but the reward is much and the Master is urgent.*

> *Nittai the Arbelite said: Keep yourself far from an evil neighbor, do not associate with the wicked.*

> *Hillel said: Do not separate yourself from the community.*

> *Shammai said: Greet all people with good cheer.*

The tombs of the Sanhedrin outside Jerusalem.

Rabbi Eleazar ben Azariah said: Where there is no Torah, there are no manners; and where there are no manners, there is no Torah. Where there is no wisdom, there is no fear; and without fear there can be no wisdom. Where there is no knowledge, there is no understanding; and without understanding there is no knowledge. Where there is no flour, there is no Torah; and where there is no Torah, there is no flour.

Rabbi Simeon said: There are three crowns—the crown of Torah, the crown of priesthood, and the crown of kingship; but the crown of a good name is above them all.

Rabbi Meir said: Look not at the bottle, look at what is in it.

20 THE JEWS OF BABYLONIA

In the ancient world, Babylonia was one of the greatest prizes for a conquerer to win. From the time the Jews were first brought to Babylonia by the Assyrians, they were given rich lands to farm. When Cyrus the Great conquered Babylonia and made it a part of the vast Persian empire, he allowed the Jews there to build synagogues and live Jewish lives. After Alexander the Great had conquered Persia, the Jews lived under the Seleucid Greek rulers, most of whom had been kind to them. And when the Parthians conquered the land from the Greeks, they took Jews into the government and allowed the Jews to trade freely as merchants. For almost 800 years, from 597 B.C.E. to 226 C.E. the Jews of Babylonia lived in peace.

The Sassanians Suddenly, in 226 C.E., the Parthians were defeated by the Sassanians of Persia. These fierce warriors carried with them a new religion, Zoroastrianism; and they tried to force all the peoples they ruled to adopt their faith in the god of light, Ohrmazd, who was said to be at war with the spirit of darkness, Ahriman. When the Jews refused to believe in two gods and refused to convert to Zoroastrianism, the Sassanians destroyed their synagogues, forced them out of the government, and made them pay heavy taxes.

The Jews might have rebelled against such treatment, but the Jewish sages of Babylonia remembered what had happened in the three wars fought against Rome in Judea. And they recalled how Yohanan ben Zakkai had saved the Jewish religion by making peace with the Romans and teaching Judaism at his school in Yavneh. So, instead of looking for a warrior-messiah or preaching that the world was about to end, the sages of Babylonia searched for a way to befriend the Sassanians.

Samuel strikes a bargain with the Sassanian ruler, Shapur.

Samuel and Rav   So it was that the famous teacher Samuel made an agreement with the Sassanian ruler Shapur I (242–272 C.E.). Samuel agreed that the Jews of Babylonia would pay taxes to Shapur, follow the laws of the land in all matters that had nothing to do with religion—in buying and selling land, for instance, and in business and trading—and would support the Sassanians in times of war. Samuel taught the Jews that the law of the land was law; and in return the Sassanian ruler allowed the Jews to rebuild their synagogues, to have their own courts, and to rule themselves. Then Samuel gathered a group of pupils at a school in Nehardea and taught them Torah and Mishnah.

At the same time, a teacher called Rav gathered pupils and built up a school at Sura. Rav had been born in Babylonia, and studied in Judea under Rabbi Judah the Prince, and taught what he had learned from the rabbis of Palestine. Both he and Samuel believed in the importance of prayer, saying that prayer was better than warfare, for God listens to prayer and hears the cries of the Jewish people to save them. And Rav taught that the study of Torah was equal to the daily sacrifices which had once been offered in the Temple of Jerusalem; and was even better than the rebuilding of the Temple itself!

Rav and Samuel raised up many great sages from among their students; and Babylonia was for a long time the most important center of Jewish learning in the world. The Jews had learned an important lesson: more can be won through friendship and peace than through warfare and all the weapons of the world. Ever after, when Jews were called upon to fight as warriors they fought with heavy hearts knowing that the cost of war is life; and that life is precious.

JEWISH LIFE IN BABYLONIA

As head of the Jewish community, a man from the line of King David was chosen to be the *Exilarch* ("Head of the Exiles"). The Jews called him the *Resh Galuta*, Aramaic for "Head of the Diaspora." Like the Patriarch in Judea, this man was the ruler of the Jews and in charge of collecting the taxes for the Sassanian kings. Often the Exilarchs were very wealthy, ruling like princes, giving feasts, and owning many slaves.

For their part, the Jews had much freedom. They were bakers and brewers (Samuel made his fortune as a brewer of beer), weavers, dyers, and tailors, blacksmiths and shipbuilders, woodcutters and porters, sailors and fishermen, farmers and merchants. Some owned carts in the marketplaces; some traded in grain, wool, precious stones, wine, and silk from the Far East.

Boys often married by the time they were eighteen; girls married even earlier. And it was not uncommon for a father to give his son a house as a wedding present. Women were given a high place among the Jews. They were in charge of educating the children; and the rabbis taught that this was one of the most important and sacred tasks in life. Women also ran the households and tended gardens. They often had rooms of their own and money for perfumes, makeup, and jewelry.

In general, life for the Jews of Babylonia was pleasant. There was time for music and laughter, for prayer and for study. And the Jewish holidays, especially Shabbat were times for joy and family sharing.

21 TALMUD: THE CROWNING GLORY

As the end of the ancient world drew near, Jewish life was ruled more and more by written laws, the teachings of the rabbis. This was true both in the rich community of Babylonia and in the poorer community of Palestine. Already in Palestine a work called the *Gemara* (from the Aramaic word for "learning") was being recorded. In the Gemara were explanations of the laws found in the Mishnah, along with other teachings of the Palestinean rabbis. Before his death in 279 C.E., Rabbi Yohanan bar Nappaha completed the final form of this Gemara; and together with the Mishnah of Rabbi Judah, it was called the Palestinean (or, sometimes, the Jerusalem) *talmud* ("teaching").

But the discussions of Rav and Samuel in Babylonia gave rise to an even greater project, the Babylonian Gemara or Talmud. Like the Palestinean Talmud, the one created in Babylonia was based on the Mishnah and included two kinds of writings. The majority of it was *Halachah* ("the way of walking," or "the path of life"). Halachah was the law of Judaism, what it meant, how it was to be followed in everyday life. It was brought together as a kind of commentary on the laws of the Mishnah.

And added to the Halachah were writings called *Aggadah* (from the word meaning "telling"). These were legends, parables, folklore, medical teachings, the lives of the rabbis, ethical teachings, teachings about astronomy and the sciences, rules of logic and thinking, and remembrances of the great teachers of the past.

The Amoraim carry on the tradition of teaching the Oral Torah.

Saboraim and Amoraim At first the Talmud of Babylonia, like the other parts of the Oral

Torah—the Mishnah and the Palestinean Gemara—was repeated by word of mouth. The students learned it by heart, repeating it over and over until it was firmly set in their memories. Then Ashi, a sage of the fifth century, collected all of the sayings and began the huge task of writing them down. After his death, Ashi's students continued to add to the Talmud, and the writing of it was finished mainly by Rabina II and those who lived after him. They were called the *Saboraim* or "Reasoners."

In size alone, the Babylonia Talmud grew to four times the length of the Palestinean Talmud, and included many of the teachings of the Palestinean rabbis. It came to be called the Talmud, and studying it became the work of a lifetime.

All the rabbis whose works and teachings were recorded in the Talmuds of Babylonia and Palestine are called the *Amoraim* or "Interpreters" because they explained to the Jews of their time the meaning of the Mishnah and the laws of the Jewish people.

A Library of Jewish Knowledge

When the Babylonian Talmud was complete, a new kind of Judaism had begun. Soon the Jewish people would be spread across the face of the earth, the Diaspora would stretch to places never dreamed of by the ancient rabbis, with strange names like Recife, Cochin, Darmstadt, York, and the like. Yet the volumes of the Talmud could be packed with their belongings, taken with them just as they carried the Tanach and the Prayerbook. The law of Judaism could be studied again and again for pleasure and entertainment, taught again and again to recall the glories of the Jewish past, interpreted again and again to help build a Jewish future. Nevermore would the teachings of the Jewish way of life be forgotten or misplaced, mistaken or blurred. From this time forward, any Jew who wanted to could open the Talmud and read it, any Jew who wished could learn the true meaning of Judaism as it was passed for thousands of years from teacher to student, from one generation to the next. Forevermore the chain of Jewish tradition would remain unbroken.

For the Jews, this was the end of the ancient world. The great covenants of the Bible had been completed by the great covenant of faithfulness. The Talmud was to be more than just a library of Jewish knowledge: it was to be the blueprint of the Jewish way of life forever.

INDEX

Aaron, 17, 21, 23
Abraham, 11–13, 26, 43
Absalom, 40–41
Aggadah, 123
Ahab (King of Israel), 47
Ahaz (King of Judah), 51
Ahriman (Zoroastrian god), 118
Akiba ben Joseph, Rabbi, 109, 112, 113
Alexander the Great (King of Macedonia), 75, 118
Alphabet (alef bet) story of, 38–39
Amoraim, 122–124
Amos (prophet), 47–48
Anthony (Mark Anthony), 83
Antigonus, 84
Antiochus IV (Epiphanes; King of Syria and Judea), 71–74, 89
Antipater, 83, 84
Anti-Semitism, religious origins of, 91
Apocrypha, 77
Aramaic language, 68
Arameans, 37
Aristobulus, 75
Ark of the Covenant, 22, 25, 32, 33, 35, 37, 41
Artaxerxes I (King of Persia), 62
Ashi, 124
Ashur, altar of, 51–52
Assyria, 48, 51–52, 55, 61, 118
Astarte (Canaanite goddess), 30, 32
Av Bet Din, 87

Baal (Caanite god), 30, 32
Babylonia
    Assyrian conquest of, 55
    captivity in, 55–56, 59, 61, 62
    Persian conquest of, 60
    Roman conquest of, 108
Babylonian Gemara, 122–125
Babylonian Jewry, 68, 97, 108, 118–120
Bar Kochba, Simeon (Simon bar Coziba), 107–111, 113
Barak (general), 29
Ben Zoma, Rabbi, 116
Benjamin, 36
Beruriah, 113
Bezalel, 23
Bible
    components of, 76–77
    See also Torah

Boaz, 45
Bet Din, 86
Bet K'nesset, 80
Bet Midrash, 80
Bet Tefillah, 80

Caleb, 24
Canaan, *see* Promised Land
Canaanites, 28, 30, 32, 33
    Babylonian, 55–56, 59–62
    Egyptian, 15, 16
Caesar, Julius (Roman emperor), 83
Christianity, 91
Circumcision
    Hadrian forbids practice of, 108–109
    as sign of covenant, 67
Covenant, 11
    circumcision as sign of, 67
    great, 20–27
Crucifixion, 89, 90
Cypros, 84
Cyrus the Great (King of Persia), 59–60, 118

Daniel (prophet), 74, 75
David (King of Israel), 36–37, 46, 49, 60, 83, 121
    reign of, 40–42
    royal line of, 44–45
Dead Sea Scrolls, 99–101
Deborah (judge), 29
Diaspora, 66–67, 96, 105, 108. 124

Egypt, 15–18, 48
    exodus from, 17–18
    Moses leaves, 15–16
    writing system in, 39
Egyptian Jewry, 96–97, 108
El (Canaanite god), 30
Eleazar ben Azariah, Rabbi, 117
Elijah (prophet), 47, 49
Elyon, El, 11
End of Days prophecy, 63
Essenes, 99, 100
Ethical monotheism, 26
Exodus, 17–18
Ezekiel (prophet), 59, 61
Ezra the Scribe, 62, 68, 78, 81, 85

First Temple, 41, 43, 51–53
    destroyed, 54–55, 57, 103
Florus, Gessius, 90, 92

Gamaliel II, Rabbi, 105, 113
Gemara, 122
   Babylonian, 122–125
Gideon (judge), 29
Golden calf worship, 21–22
Goliath, 44
Great Assembly, 68–69, 81, 87

Hadrian (Roman emperor), 108, 110,
   113
Haggai (prophet), 62
Halachah, 123
Hanina ben Dosa, 103
Hasidism, 66–70, 74, 78
Hebrew language, 39
   Aramaic and Greek supplant, 67,
   68
Hellenism, 66–70
Herod (King of Judea), 83–86, 94
Hezekiah (King of Judah), 52–53
Hillel, Rabbi, 79, 80, 86, 87, 99, 102,
   105, 116
Hiram (King of Tyre), 41
Holy Scriptures, see Bible
Hyeroglyphic writing system, 39
Hyrcanus (King of Judea), 75, 83, 84

Independence, War of, 99
Isaac, 11, 12, 43
Isaiah (prophet), 51–53, 63
Israel, Kingdom of (Northern
   Kingdom), 46–48, 50

Jacob, 11, 43
Jehoiakim (King of Judah), 53–55
Jeremiah (prophet), 54–56
Jeroboam (King of Israel), 46
Jesse, 36, 44
Jesus of Nazareth, 89–91
Jethro, 16, 20
Jonathan, 37
Joseph, 15
Josephus, 92, 98
Joshua, 24, 25, 28, 32, 81
Joshua, Rabbi, 104
Josiah (King of Judah), 53
Judah, Kingdom of, 50–57
   end of, 54–57
Judah the Prince, 113–114, 120, 122
Judea, Kingdom of
   languages used in, 68
   last days of, 89–95
   See also specific kings
Judges, 29, 31–32

Ketuvim, 76–77

Maccabee, Judah, 72–73, 75
Maccabee, Simon, 75
Manna, 20
Mariamne, 84, 86
Marcus Aurelius (Roman emperor),
   114
Masada, 94, 95
Mattathias, 72
Matzah, 17
Meir, Rabbi, 113, 117
Menasseh (King of Judah), 53
Mesorah, 81
   See also Pharisees
Messiah, as descendant of David, 45
Micah (prophet), 50
Midianites, 29
Midrash, 103
Miriam the Prophetess, 18
Mishnah, 114–115, 122–124
Monotheism, 13, 26
Moses, 15–19, 21–25, 28, 53, 61, 69,
   78, 81, 96

Nahum (prophet), 53
Naomi, 44
Nasi, 87
Nathan (prophet), 41
Nebuchadnezzar (Assyrian king), 55,
   56, 59, 74
Neco (Egyptian pharaoh), 53
Nevi'im, 76
Nehemiah, 62, 85
Nero (Roman emperor), 92, 104
Nittai the Arbelite, Rabbi, 116

Octavian (Roman emperor), 83, 85,
   86
Ohrmazd (Zoroastrian god), 118
Oral Torah, 78–81, 114
   See also Mishnah; Talmud

Palestine, Romans rename Judea, 94
Palestinean Talmud, 122–124
Paul of Tarse, 91
Persia, 89, 118
Pharisees, 101
   and Hadrian's prohibitions,
   108–109
   Herod and, 86
   importance of teaching to, 103
   and Jesus of Nazareth, 90, 91
   Saduccees and, 76–81
   and war against Rome, 92
Philistines, 31–33, 35–37, 44
Philo, 96–97
Phoenicians, 38–39, 41

Pirke Akvot, 116
Pilate, Pontius, 89–91
Plato, 96
Pompey, 75, 83
Procurators, Roman, 89
Promised land (Canaan), 21
   exodus toward, 17–18
   fighting for, 28–33
   spies sent into, 24–25
Publicans, 89

Rabbis, 102–105
   Hadrian and, 113
   See also specific rabbis
Rabina II, Rabbi, 124
Rav, Rabbi, 120, 123
Rebecca, 15
Rebohoam (King of Judah), 46
Resh Galuta, 121
Roman legions, 89
Rome, 75, 89, 100
   Bar Kochba rebellion against,
      107–111, 113
   Herod and, 83–86
   Masada battle, 94
   war against, 90, 92, 94, 98, 101, 118
   See also specific emperors
Rural life under King Solomon's
   reign, 43
Ruth, 44–45

Sabbath, Sadduccean and Pharisean
   positions on breaking, 78, 80
Saboraim, 123–124
Sadducees, 76–81, 86, 92, 103
Salome, 86
Samaritans, 61
Samson, 31
Samuel (judge), 35, 36
Samuel, Rabbi, 120, 122
Sanhedrin, 86, 87, 117
   Yavneh, 105, 109, 113, 118
Sassanians, 118
Saul (King of Israel), 36–37
Second Isaiah (prophet), 59, 63
Second Temple, 60, 71, 85–86, 93
   dedication of, 62, 73
   destruction of, 94, 97, 98, 101, 104,
      105
Sennacherib (Assyrian king), 53
Septuagint, 67
Shalmaneser (Assyrian king), 48
Shammai, Rabbi, 79, 80, 86, 99, 116
Shapur (Persian king), 118, 120
Shemitah, 33

Shiloh sanctuary, 23, 32, 33
Simeon, Rabbi, 117
Simon, Rabbi, 113, 114
Sinai, Mount (Mount Horeb), 16, 18,
   20, 21, 26, 29
Sisera (general), 29
Solomon (King of Israel), 41–43, 46,
   49, 55, 76
Stoics, 96
Synagogues
   Babylonian, 97, 118, 119
   concept of, 70
   defined, 66
   Egyptian, 97
   Pharisees and, 80, 101

Talmud
   Babylonian Gemara, 122–125
   Palestinean, 122, 124
Tannaim, 103
   See also Pharisees
Tarphon, Rabbi, 116
Temple, the, *see* First Temple;
   Second Temple
Ten commandments, 21, 26–27
Tiglathpileser (Assyrian king), 48, 51
Titus (Roman emperor), 92
Torah, 17, 21, 25, 53, 58, 76, 80, 91,
   94, 101
   Aramaic translation of, 68
   Greek translations of, 67
   schools set up to teach, 105; *see
      also* Pharisees
   See also Oral Torah
Trajan (Roman emperor), 98, 107, 108
Tzaddik, 114

Uriah (prophet), 54

Valley of the Bones prophecy, 61
Vespasian (Roman emperor), 92,
   103–104

Yavneh Sanhedrin, 105, 109, 113, 118
Yonahan bar Nappaha, Rabbi, 123
Yonahan ben Zakkai, Rabbi,
   102–105, 118
Yovel, 33

Zadok, 76
Zealots (Sicarii), 89, 92, 94, 98–101,
   103, 108
Zechariah (prophet), 62
Zedekiah (King of Judah), 55
Zeus (Jupiter; Greek and Roman god), 71
Zoroastrianism, 100–101, 118